Amanda Thomson is a Sco............... ...u visual artist, and a lecturer at the Glasgow School of Art. Her first book, *A Scots Dictionary of Nature*, was published in 2018. She has spoken at many book festivals and had her work published in *Antlers of Water*, *Willowherb Review*, *The Wild Isles*, *Gifts of Gravity and Light* and the *Guardian*. She lives and works in Strathspey in the Scottish Highlands and Glasgow.

@passingplace | passingplace.com

'An evocative, intimate journey through the ways we find home – in family, place, history and language'
JESSICA J. LEE

'Amanda Thomson brings a careful and a thoughtful attention to the page'
MALACHY TALLACK

'A finely-wrought meditation on nature, identity and the tender hold of the past'
SAMANTHA WALTON

'Strikingly original . . . Thomson crafts a cadence that is as wise as it is vitally alive'
MARGOT DOUAIHY

Also by Amanda Thomson

A Scots Dictionary of Nature

belonging

Natural
histories of
place, identity
and home

AMANDA
THOMSON

CANONGATE

This paperback edition published by Canongate Books in 2023

First published in Great Britain in 2022
by Canongate Books Ltd,
14 High Street, Edinburgh EH1 1TE

canongate.co.uk

1

Extract from 'A Man is Assynt' by Norman MacCaig, written c. 1967.
First published by Chatto & Windus in 1970 in *A Man in My Position*.
Published in *The Poems of Norman MacCaig* (Polygon, 2005).
Reproduced by permission of Polygon, an imprint of Birlinn.

For image credits please see p. 311

For more information about this book and
Amanda Thomson please visit: passingplace.com

British Library Cataloguing-in-Publication Data
A catalogue record for this book is available on
request from the British Library

ISBN 978 1 83885 474 4

Typeset in Bembo by Palimpsest Book Production Ltd,
Falkirk, Stirlingshire

Printed and bound in Great Britain by Clays Ltd, Elcograf S.p.A.

*For Mum and for Elizabeth, with me
every step of the way*

understory   the (layer of) vegetation growing beneath the level of the tallest trees in a forest

snag

1. a standing dead tree. Deadwood is vital for the sustained health of a forest
2. that which catches our attention, emotionally resonates; that which catches and holds us, often momentarily and sometimes surreptitiously

Prologue

OUT OF PLACE

IN THE BACK GREEN OF my mum's house stand two rowan trees I've known since childhood. At first, I'd just be able to reach up and touch the lowest branch. Later, I'd grasp it to swing myself up into the tree. It broke or was sawn off years ago now, and the trees themselves are old and feel frail, brittle. Any time there's a storm or high winds, my mum worries that branches will break off and knock out the telephone line or, worse, batter onto the roof.

The rowan is a folkloric tree in Scotland; they've been used in medicine, to dye clothes, and are thought to ward off evil spirits and protect against disease. At our house in the Highlands we've planted two rowan trees, one on each side of the gate leading into the field. If they take, they will outlive us, and at one point, they might provide some protection from the wind. At the back of the house and up a hill is a small stand of four granny pines, which I always think of as our coven, standing watch over the house, which is made of larch. Abernethy Forest in Strathspey is a place I've been making artwork about for some years, and it's where I'm now lucky to live. It has been described as an important remnant of ancient Caledonian pinewoods, and holds the most extensive area of these woods in Scotland. For many, it's a stunning, heart-stopping place to be.

There's a lovely phrase about the Caledonian pinewoods of Scotland that resonates with me every time I walk within them – 'to stand in them is to feel the past'. It's from a book written in the late 1950s, *The Native Pinewoods of Scotland*, by H.M. Steven, then Professor of Forestry at Aberdeen University, and A. 'Jock' Carlisle. They write: 'The trees range in age up to 300 years in some instances, and there are thus not very many generations between their earliest predecessors about 9,000 years ago and those growing today.'[1] To talk about a general timelessness in these forests is somewhat clichéd, but to consider how our very particular human time rubs up with such longevity is something else entirely.

At the back of my mum's house, right at the border, a conifer looms taller than the house, casting its shadow over the green. One summer, jackdaws terrorised a blackbirds' nest and the garden was in a constant state of agitation. The daughter of our upstairs neighbours planted that conifer when she was a child, after it had served its purpose as a Christmas tree in their house. She's now in her seventies.

Early on in my walks through the Scots pinewoods of Abernethy, I began to notice the standing dead trees. They come in all shapes and sizes, barkless and pale amongst the deep greens of the living trees, pockmarked, riddled with the traces of beetles and beasties; some retain their bark, some are lichen-covered. Over time they will fracture their branches, sometimes shear half their trunks onto the forest floor. Such trees are known as snags, and when I investigated further, I found that deadwood in a Scots pine forest is incredibly important for the forest's health. These trees can stand for decades, decaying quietly, slowly, leaching a gradual and steady release of nutrients back into the forest's understory. They are home to a vast array of birds and insects, some very rare – specialist saproxylic species, including several types of beetles, wasps and hoverflies – and the lichens and fungi are dependent on these microhabitats – ecological islands of otherness – that dead and dying wood provides. Birds nest in their hollows and holes, and eat the insects that feed on the dead wood. I love the idea that the dead can sustain the living, and it has become an important touchstone for me – how that which is no longer with us can make us who we are and can be a continuous source of strength or comfort.

We see different types of snags all over Scotland. Standing stones and other prehistoric relics dot the landscape and we'll sometimes come across the remains of Clearance villages and the shells of old crofts and sheilings. Closer to now lies evidence of more recent histories: paths that were once railway lines; factories and mills and churches now turned into housing and offices; an industrial crane that has been kept as a symbol of a city's ship-building past, that some will still remember in use. But we also have old letters, documents and photographs with, if we are lucky, names and dates and

3

places written on the back. We have the National Records of Scotland and ancestry.co.uk. We drive past places that we used to visit, where people we know used to stay, or we return to places we've not been in a while, and something is evoked, or provoked, in us. Such things are testaments to earlier days and moments in our lives.

The snag is one of the understories of this book. It's also a great word. It can be something that catches our attention, emotionally resonates, arrests and holds us, often momentarily and sometimes surreptitiously. Although the word can have negative connotations, I think of snags as hooks on which we can hang past experiences that remind us of the disparate moments and aspects of our lives that have made us who we are, who we have become. In an old Scots language dictionary, a snag is a branch that has been completely broken from a tree, and I wonder about the continuity and disjuncture from our past that is a part of how our lives move on. I wonder how the dead, the things that are no longer with us, continue not just to influence but give succour to the present. Perhaps that's always been a concern of mine. The first artwork I made after discovering these Scots pine snags and their significance was called *dead amongst the living*. It started as a documentation of the dead trees that I encountered in a small area near the house I was staying in, and it's become about the lives being lived around them still.

Is there a word for the fear of forgetting?

PART I

mind   a memory; a reminder; affection. (v) to remember; to remember in a will; to remind; to notice; to take care of; to have a mind to; to wish.

minding   recollection[2]

WHEN I WAS A CHILD, growing up in the 1970s and '80s in a small, working-class Scottish town to the northeast of Glasgow, my mum, gran, papa and I would go for walks on Sunday afternoons. The paths we chose took us out of the town and into the countryside. We'd walk up the road and cross through a gap in a fence beyond what was called the Big Stane, a large boulder that all the local kids would use as a slide, and down over the Couches, (pronounced *cootchies*), a hilly moorland that sat between the scheme where we stayed and the Stirling Road. We'd walk along a disused railway track to Colzium Estate – to Colzium House, a formerly grand old house originally built in the eighteenth century that is surrounded by gardens and woods – or to Banton Loch, locally known as the dam.

From the start, family has been bound to my experience of nature. Some birds remind me of childhood, still. When I hear the song of a summer skylark I think of going to pick blaeberries with my mum and gran over the Couches; speugs (house sparrows) remind me of my gran and papa and how they fed them stale plain bread in the back garden; and I remember blue tits pecking through the foil top of the milk bottle left at the front door every morning. I learned to see if rain was coming by looking out over the hills to the north and watching the clouds for the wind's direction. From our living room, we'd see skeins of geese flying along the line of them, signalling a change of season. Birdwatching as a hobby came to me in my early teens, and to this day, memories of places are often linked to a specific bird seen on a particular day and sometimes to an unusual light or weather.

One of the first bird books I ever got was *Highland Birds*, by Desmond Nethersole-Thompson. First published in 1971, the unbridled, almost breathless enthusiasm of his writing bemused me, but his vast knowledge and love of the Highlands was clear. I must have got it in John Smith's, a multi-storey bookshop that used to be on St Vincent Street in Glasgow city centre, which I still remember for its nooks and different stairwells that took you to odd levels. It was always a destination when my mum took me into town. She'd let me wander and then buy me a book. Nethersole-Thompson took me to places that, to my Lowland Scots self of that time, seemed impossibly distant, to landscapes I longed to discover and a list of birds I craved, and still love, to see. Eagles and ospreys, capers and crossbills, divers and corncrakes. It was only in 2018 that I finally saw a red-necked phalarope, on Unst, in Shetland. I'll always associate the pinewoods of Rothiemurchus around Loch an Eilein with crested tits – the first place I ever saw them, when on a Young Ornithologists' Club holiday in my teens. My first sighting of a golden eagle – being mobbed by peregrines – was at Glen Tilt as a teenager, on that same holiday, and even now those raptors and that sunny day and blue sky and the long wide glen are all bound together for me.

Loch an Eilein and Rothiemurchus hold a memory of a cuckoo I heard and saw in early summer when walking the approach towards the Lairig Ghru. The cuckoo flew from birch tree to fence post to birch – its call the only indication of its presence until it moved. Now, not that many miles northeast as the crow flies, I'll expect to hear the first cuckoos in the last week of April and see them sitting on the wires outside the house as May spills into June.

I have seen red-throated divers off the coast of Achmelvich and restless charms of linnets on the wires above the car park there. A little further north, a great northern diver preened and dived close into the shore of the bay at Clachtoll, so close I could see the black and white stripes of its neck collar and its intricate flash in the morning of an early autumn day. The previous squally afternoon was spent leaning into the wind, watching gannets plunge into the froth of a tempestuous sea at

Stoer Point. Once, on holiday, we took a winter's walk along the banks of the Spey and a peregrine falcon plummeted into a bundle of finches, scattering them like confetti, and though it's been almost two decades, I remember that walk and that day each time I pass by that spot.

My interests in place and nature have always motivated my work as an artist and writer, and more recently they have become entangled with questions of family, belonging, landscape and home. The processes of making art and writing are fascinating and mysterious to me. What grabs and holds you? What sits with you and becomes a story, or an essay, or an etching? How do we make sense of the seemingly disparate parts of life, connecting past to present, or one year to the next? Sometimes you don't know what details will linger in your mind or what will resonate, or the connections you might make. When I came across an old nineteenth-century *Jamieson's Dictionary of the Scottish Language* in a second-hand bookshop, I didn't immediately know where it would take me, and yet it was here I started to gather Scots words about aspects of place that helped me find another way into thinking and making work about places, forests and trees. This resulted in my own book, *A Scots Dictionary of Nature*, where I gathered together Scots words for weather, birds, the land, water, wood and walking.

As a printmaker, I use old techniques like etching and lithography where ideas become realised over a period of time and via a number of processes. Printmaking is a slow art, and often I never quite know what the final result will be until I lift the paper from the press bed. I teach too, and one of the things I often say to my students is that sometimes the art that works best doesn't answer questions but provides an openness that makes others ask questions or helps us see in new or different ways. I most enjoy, and am often most compelled by, art and writing that complicates, shatters, reconstructs, but doesn't necessarily provide any or all the answers. Art that shows unexpected connections or perhaps asks us to join the dots from our own experiences, between the varying fragments of our own lives, and every now and again, to see where the gaps are, and learn from them. Just as it's important for us as writers and artists to define the stories we want to tell, and the spaces that we find to tell them. 'Spaces can be real and imagined,' writes bell hooks. 'Spaces can tell stories and unfold histories. Spaces can be interrupted, appropriated and transformed through artistic and literary practice.'[3] And it can be enough to write around and about these spaces without having answers, without having to qualify, or justify, or give solace or explanation or solutions. Spaces shapeshift; they alter depending on where you stand, with the changing light and with the shadows cast. Spaces can be monumental or tiny, and the tiny can feel monumental. And while it's important to recognise that spaces can represent invisibility and erasure, and assumptions of solidity and presence can be erased, spaces can also be reclaimed.

As I get older and my life lengthens, those I have known and the early encounters and experiences that shaped me are moving further away. People fade. Places recede from view. The old words I found in the nineteenth-century dictionary (re) minded me of my grandparents and their generation, all long gone, and of my family and the town and environs where I grew up. Accent and words have, in part, been 'educated' out of me, or become lost through time and circumstance. Some words I found pulled towards me fragments of my own memories and my mum would point out words she had not heard or used in years. The process of gathering old Scots words started me thinking about the past and about my family in a way that I wanted to delve deeper into. My mum sought out old photographs and papers that had sat in drawers and envelopes and old Quality Street tins for a lifetime, and we started to go through them together.

It's obvious, perhaps, that when making art or writing you bring with you your interests, experiences and perceptions. Sometimes, as I walk, I'm an artist at work and at other times I'm a birdwatcher or hillwalker. The artist is left at the door and nothing comes of the experience, bar the experience itself, which is often more than enough. I also carry the knowledge and experiences of my childhood years and beyond as I go through my life. Each of us has different identities and interests that ebb and flow depending on where we are, what we are doing, the questions we hold and, perhaps, questions that the land and others ask of us.

Intersectionality is a concept first coined by US law professor Kimberlé Crenshaw over thirty years ago.[4] It refers to how one's race, class, gender, age, sexuality, disability and ethnicity may combine, and sometimes exist in tension, to shape one's experience of the world, how one is perceived in it, and the power and inequality one might experience at different times and in different contexts. It is, arguably, a hifalutin term, but it's an important one for me, because a lot of what I am thinking about is what has made me who I am and what defines me – indeed how we all are, and become, defined. Sometimes I have to choose between boxes that may or may not include ovo-lacto vegetarian/Black British/Black Scottish/ mixed ethnicity/gay/civilly partnered; and I wonder what might be inferred about who I am, what I am like. 'Definitions belong to the definers, not the defined,' writes Toni Morrison.[5]

When I am walking up a hill, or cooking dinner, I'm not usually thinking in such categories. Even if I am dwelling on something, walking, the landscape, weather, birds, will pull me out of myself. Or I'll go into my headspace or the music or podcasts I am listening to, or whatever is preoccupying my mind at that time, which is occasionally racism, occasionally homophobia, but often it's only if something has caused these things to be present, something that I have to react to. More often than not, I'll be thinking about something I've read or been talking about, or I'll have a tune going through my head. Occasionally I'll be in a state of general or work-related anxiousness, or wondering what my partner and I are going to do at the weekend, or what that birdcall might be, or I'll float along thinking about nothing in particular.

Megan/Morgan, one of the characters in Bernardine Evaristo's Booker Prize-winning *Girl, Woman, Other*, talks about how they'd been asked to write a memoir, and declined. 'They didn't really want to write hurtful things about their family, the angle the publishers were after, a "how I triumphed over a painful childhood" number.'[6] I hadn't necessarily articulated it before, but it strikes me that this same curiosity, sometimes expectation, occasionally a demand, for information (sometimes in something as innocuous as 'where are you from?') has often trailed me as I've gone through life in ways that it hasn't for others, and there's been an expectation of some kind of tale of woe. Often I've found that what people perceive as having to be the defining factor about me is my colour and my dreadlocks – that which is most visible. But identity is invisible as well as visible, and it can be what you hold to your heart. Notions of it are slippery and relational, as are notions of home, and in this complicated web we find out who and what we are, and who and what make us who we are. I think of what Anthony Anaxagorou says of race and racism in his wonderful collection, *After the Formalities*: 'Everything's already been said much better by people who had it much worse.'[7]

Though it's clear that stories of discriminations, small and large, still need telling, repeating, over and over, until they are heard and properly understood. Questions of difference and discrimination can often relate to what it is to feel at, to be at, home. What are the conditions that make you feel safe and secure? What is it to long for something? What is it to belong?

I am someone who's wholly enthralled and intrigued by the landscapes of Scotland, and different parts of me are interwoven throughout this country. Perhaps it's only now that I've given myself permission to be myself and to think about where I've settled, where I belong. I've never been one to keep a journal or a diary, not beyond my teenage years anyway, and during a purge years ago I threw out most of my old letters, photographs and any diaries that I still had. So when I think back, I have years that I don't remember or years that blend into others. I know if I was cored like a tree there would be some years that would reveal more stress and anxiety, and others that would reveal more joy. Not having children, I don't have the rites of passage that some have in relation to their ageing, and now that I'm trying to remember, I feel like I've forgotten so much.

The Covid-19 pandemic unleashed a wholly different kind of precarity that I, and most of Scotland, Europe, the world, had never before experienced or expected. Questions of home, belonging, access and safety took on altogether different meanings and resonances. In Scotland and elsewhere, access to going outside, or visiting family – never mind travelling about the country, something we've always taken for granted – took on a different poignancy and meaning.

From my landlocked lockdowned home in the Highlands I watched online the Black Lives Matter protests and uprisings in US cities and the corresponding actions of solidarity across the world after the murders of George Floyd, Breonna Taylor and others at the hands of the police, which brought to the fore, once again, these complex, urgent and long-standing questions about racism, discrimination, ownership and responsibility. I watched Covid spread and morph into different variants; Brexit; the end of the Trump presidency; the unending legacies and realities of conflicts across the world, and the continual trauma of those fleeing conflict and their own homes to seek safety and a new place to call home; and others whose homes through conflict, or the effects of climate change, became no longer safe. All raise questions about different kinds of precarity that some have always had to think about more than others, and I know how lucky I am to be where I am.

Often I find myself thinking about what it is to care about land and about people – what is here, what has been, what we're moving towards. And this is really what b*elonging* is about. It's about noticing and caring and taking stock. It's also about home, and what makes us feel at home, and the different things that home can be. Toni Morrison asks, 'How do we decide where we belong? What convinces us that we do?'[8]

The world is, of course, constantly changing, and as I walk in nature I'm intrigued by some of the not-knowing that also lives within what we recognise, know and understand and by our capacity to always learn more. Nan Shepherd, in *The Living Mountain*, wrote of a child who had said to her 'I like the unpath best',[9] and it seems to me that those moments of unprescribed discovery in somewhat familiar places are often what we remember and recall most vividly. At the same time, context, experience and who we are in the world counts a lot for where we are, what we see and what we understand. 'Knowledge does not dispel mystery,' Shepherd wrote. Sometimes, in coming to know new places, new things, you begin to reflect on other, older places, people and interactions, and these can be the smallest or seemingly insignificant instances or fragments, barely remembered. We try to make sense of them, find narratives, try to identify that which has pulled us in, the things that have snagged us and stuck with us. Beth Loffreda and Claudia Rankine, in *The Racial Imaginary*, said that 'writing could be said to rest on the faith that there is something of value in witnessing an individual mind speaking in and to its ordinary history. This never stops.'[10] So I'll write my own *ordinary history* and somewhere along the way try to find and define my own belonging, my own place *here*, whatever and wherever that *here* may be.

houris the chanting of birds

The song of tree pipits, willow warblers and, perhaps, a redstart, all newly arrived; great tits, chaffinches in call and response, and the sound of distant geese still on the loch.

WHEN I WAS DOING MY undergrad degree at art school, I made a large etching that I called *Zugunruhe*. I'd come across the term in a book by Scott Weidensaul, *Living on the Wind: Across the Hemisphere with Migratory Birds*. *Zugunruhe* is a German word which means a migratory restlessness, and Weidensaul writes: 'It describes the nocturnal restlessness that European birdkeepers noticed centuries ago in their caged nightingales and other captive songbirds. In spring and fall, the birds began fluttering in their cages just before sunset, continuing until a few hours after midnight – the same period, it turns out, as the peak of nocturnal migration each night.'[11]

It reminds me of the Scots phrase *nicht-hawk*, 'someone who ranges about at night', a more local flightiness, and it makes me think of the swallows that arrive to join the others who've been around all summer to congregate on the wires outside the house every August. You can almost feel their un-settling, their need to untether grow. You can sense them gearing up for their long journey south again.

To make *Zugunruhe,* I asked people who came from a wide variety of places to write about their journeys home. Some wrote physically about travelling, through airports and along streets, and others wrote more metaphorically. I took fragments of their words and made them into a map of the world, their words and the lines of the pages they wrote making the contours and the borders, fragments that never quite told anyone's whole story. And yet together, they made a map of home and movement and the world.

I GREW UP IN A TOWN called Kilsyth, about fifteen miles northeast of Glasgow, in the Kelvin Valley. I probably spent my entire childhood in the Central Belt, apart from two weeks every summer when we went to a caravan on the East Coast. The Kelvin, the second major river that runs through Glasgow, starts its journey at Kelvinhead, about four miles east of Kilsyth. Just south of the town and beyond the Kelvin runs the Forth and Clyde Canal, which opened in 1790 and connected the River Clyde and Glasgow in the west to the Firth of Forth and Edinburgh in the east. In its nineteenth- and early twentieth-century heyday, it was an important trade route between the two coasts and beyond. This town holds the first of my snags. I can trace myself from there, and thereabouts, and it's the earlier generations of my mum's family on her mother's side – the Taylors – that I remember and hold closest in my life. Growing up, I lived with my mum, gran and papa, a 'mixed-race' girl in a white family, a white town. Gay too, though I wouldn't have named it, didn't even consider it when I lived there. When I think of home I think of our house, this family and this place.

It's an old town, small, with a population of around 10,000. Older histories of Kilsyth tend to be written by its ministers, though the town itself is not as God-fearing as it once was. Its coat of arms consists of crossed swords, a bible, a shuttle and a miner's lamp, speaking to its past industries and histories. This was the badge on our school blazers, with the town's motto, *Spe Expecto* (I Look Forward in Hope) embroidered beneath. I much prefer the motto of the next town west, Kirkintilloch, which is in Scots – *Ca' Canny But Ca' Awa* – and means, depending on who you ask, 'progress with vigilance' or 'take care but do it anyway'.

Kilsyth, Stirlingshire, 1898

In 1645, the Battle of Kilsyth, fought between Royalists and Covenanters, took place on the site where Banton Loch is now. Francis H. Groome in his *Ordnance Gazetteer of Scotland*, published in 1885, quotes the Reverend Mr Robert Rennie (from the *Old Statistical Account*), who says of the battle:

Suffice it to say, that every little hill and valley bears the name, or records the deeds of that day; so that the situation of each army can be distinctly traced. Such as the Bullet and Baggage Knowe, the Drum Burn, the Slaughter Howe or hollow, Kill-e-many Butts, etc., etc. In the Bullet Knowe and neighbourhood bullets are found every year, and in some places so thick that you may lift three or four without moving a step. In the Slaughter Howe, and a variety of other places, bones and skeletons may be dug up everywhere; and in every little bog or marsh for 3 miles, especially in the Dullatur Bog, they have been discovered in almost every ditch. The places where the bodies lie in any number may be easily known; as the grass is always of a more luxuriant growth in summer, and of a yellowish tinge in spring and harvest.[12]

Had we known that aspect of the battle as kids, we'd have been all over these places looking for bullets and bones and yellowing grass. As it was, we made our own histories and games, and walked and played in these places unaware of those who still lay beneath.

The remains of the Roman-built Antonine Wall runs in an east–west line just south of the town, and just south of where the Forth and Clyde Canal now runs. That is also to say, just south of where my great- and great-great-grandfathers were blacksmiths and bridge-keepers on the canal at Auchinstarry.

Kilsyth was a solidly working-class town that in the nineteenth, and into the twentieth, century was known for weaving and mining. Across from the old Victorian primary school, which my cousins and I remember for its bicycle sheds and the rats that scuthered under floorboards, was Shuttle Street, and I can vaguely remember the line of white weavers' cottages found there, though they were demolished when I was still at primary school.

In the 1970s, it was a small-ish, insular-ish place. Perhaps it still is, but today more people have moved here from other places, with the idea of living closer to the countryside and commuting to work in Glasgow, Edinburgh or Stirling. In earlier days, Kilsyth had two railway stations, and paths still known as the high line and the low line take us across and out of the town and into the countryside beyond.

I was brought up in the house where my mum still stays. It's a bottom corner flat in one of these roughcast, four-flat-per-block council houses that went up between the wars (as if there has only been two). It's number 13, which I've always held as a lucky number, and that must say something about how I view my childhood. Before they moved there, my mum and her two sisters, my gran and papa stayed in the end house of a terrace less than half a mile away. When I was at school, I would go into that house occasionally, visiting a childhood friend whose family lived there, long after mine. It must have occurred to me when I visited her that I was sometimes standing in the very room where my mother was born.

At the time my family lived there, they were without an inside bathroom and had to go to 'the lavvy' at the gable end, which they shared with their neighbours. My papa dug a long herbaceous border behind the house – the only garden as such – and some of the plants there were taken up to the house where my mum still stays. Some of the flowers from her garden are now with me here in the Highlands. Other details about the Low Craigends house are sometimes carved out as my mum talks about people she remembers: 'We didn't have a cooker. We had a gas hob which was about that depth' – she holds her hand horizontal about a foot and a half from the floor – 'and it sat on the floor next to the fireplace, and when it wasn't in use there was a wee chair that sat on top of it. Quite a low wee chair with wee arms. And Auntie Maggie would come in and sit on that chair and get a cup of tea. And she always sat like that' – my mum demonstrates – 'one leg crossed and tucked under the other . . . I always waited for her to sit down and put her legs like that. She was a lovely wee sowl.'

They swapped that house with another family, as my grandparents' family grew and moved to where my mum lives now. I'm not sure why the family they swapped with wanted to swap to somewhere with no inside loo. My family moved when my mum was about fourteen, so she has been in her current house for seventy years, give or take. To this day, I still say I'm going home when I'm going to Kilsyth.

My mum's house sits in the older part of the town, and one of my cousins stays just down the road in what used to be her (my cousin's) paternal grandparents' house. It was an old farmhouse back in the day, and my mum remembers as a little girl going with my gran to buy the sour milk they sold from their outhouse, to make scones. My cousin's house is surrounded by mostly (ex-)council houses now, ours included. My mum has a black-and-white photograph of her and her sisters sitting on the wall at the back of the Low Craigends house when my mum was about twelve, and behind them are just fields, stretching all the way to what is now my cousin's home.

We still have the small shed up the back, which my papa, who died in 1982, built when they moved there. It came from somewhere else too. His wicker fishing basket is still on a shelf, and there are supports in the roof that used to hold his old cane fishing rods but now hold my old rusted Swingball. The drawers he built for his tools now hold Mum's gardening secateurs and forks. Attached to the rough workbench he would also have made is a massive cast-iron vice, which my uncle remembers him somehow carrying back from the Barras in Glasgow on the bus. I remember playing in the shed and climbing the fence behind it to get up onto the roof in order to jump off.

In the front garden, an old, not that long dead stub of a golden privet sits to the left of the stairs up to the house. My mum says it grew as a result of her maternal grandfather – Grandpa Taylor – coming to visit and removing the twig he had in his bunnet and sticking it into the soil. Its children are still dotted around, and at the top of the stairs a royal fern still thrives. It has followed the family from house to house to house, and must now be over a hundred years old. I remember driving toy cars through it when I was a child. Also growing is some yellow loosestrife from my Aunt Mary's garden at the Haggs – the house in Castleview Terrace where my Aunt Mary, really my Great-Aunt Mary (my gran's sister) lived until she died in her eighties. Another plant comes from my (Great-) Aunt Liz, my gran's oldest sister, who stayed in Dennyloanhead and made the best treacle toffee in the world. The quince tree that climbs up the back wall has been there for as long as I can remember too, and has fruit that comes and goes which we never ever do anything with. Four rusted cast-iron clothes poles – two at either end – frame the back green and used to make perfect goalposts, and the two rowans that my mum remembers as having the same girth as her arm when they moved in are by the fence shared by the neighbouring block. It sounds like it's a big place, a big garden, but it's not. It's modest, council house-sized. As a child, it felt big, big enough, though as a teenager, not so much.

I get the feeling that this family of mine, the Taylors and the Thomsons, have tended to stay in one place, or close by, for a long time – most of us, at least. It seems we're resolutely from across the Central Belt. When I say *we*, I'm talking matrilineally, which is who I always think of when I think of family. We are quite sedentary, when it comes down to it, although, like my mum before me, I've pushed out a little more: Edinburgh for university, Madrid for a little after that, then Glasgow, Chicago for a couple of years, back to Glasgow and here to Strathspey, which I reckon will hold me. I think I come from a modest place and from modest stock, with modest, contained lives, perhaps unremarkable, but then so many of us come from these kinds of lives and histories.

From an early age I've always interacted with nature and the countryside without necessarily knowing it. Nature was just what I knew. That's not to say that I was one of those kids who knew the names of flowers or all the birds and insects. Rather, when I was younger, it was within nature that I played: we went to the burn to catch tadpoles, played and rolled down the hills, went for walks, and foretold the day's weather by looking west over the hills. Nature, though I didn't quite realise it then, was always close, just there. I was in the middle of it without knowing there could be anything else. On Sunday afternoons after church and the stew we always had for dinner (which now would be called lunch), me, my mum, gran and papa would go for a walk – what my gran called a dauner – and encounter what felt like half the town out doing the same. We'd walk along the canal or around the dam and up to Colzium House and gardens and up through the bluebell woods to a small shelter called the Granny's Mutch, and walk home via the high line. A mutch, I know now, is an old Scots word for a linen hat, and the shelter is indeed shaped like a bonnet, with a semi-circular dome. It was built probably a century and a half ago for people to sit and contemplate the waterfall that tumbles down beside it. Today, it is covered in graffiti and no longer has its seat. It feels like we meet fewer people out for walks, and some of the paths seem more overgrown.

Kilsyth was the kind of place where we talked about going 'up the glen' – without realising that glen was a general Scots word for ravine. It's the Garrel Glen which holds the Garrel burn that runs from the hills down through Kilsyth, eventually joining the River Kelvin just south of the town. The Glen starts above the town, has a set of caves used by the Covenanters, holds deep pools you can swim in, and goes up and into the Kilsyth Hills, all the way up to the Laird's Loup, which we could see from the living room of our house, on the horizon, in the dip between the hills.

The glen, the dam: singular places to go to, and early on I never thought of there being multiple glens, multiple dams. Still, even now, if my mum talks about shopping, we go 'down the street'. Singular. It's the kind of place where the road that comes over the hills from Stirling is called the Tak Ma Doon

Road and where many families have been in the town, or thereabouts, for generations, my own family included. It feels like there's been a continuity that's maybe breaking more these days. My mum and her generation, who've been in the town most of their lives, who went to school there, can bump into people they've known since childhood and trace multiple stories and connections across generations. I left there at eighteen, and there's a rupture and a distance between me and the broader story of the town and who's there, who's left, those I used to know at school.

I ask my mum about the name 'Couches' and she thinks it comes from the French. I discover they were named in the early 1800s when the land, after being common pasture, was enclosed and, after a further dispute, divided up into individual parcels called lazy beds.[13] On the way to the canal from our house is a steep hill that locals call 'Mal Fleemin's Brae' that takes you down to the Coach Road. It's the road that would take folk down to the wharves that used to be at the canal at Auchinstarry. Mal Fleming was the carter who helped pull loads back up to the town at this point of the journey.[14]

The Kilsyth Hills, writes Groome in the late nineteenth century, are 'picturesquely intersected with short deep glens and commands, from its loftiest summits, magnificent views from sea to sea, and over parts of fourteen counties'.[15] And yes, looking east from Tamtain, the highest of the hills and where the Tak Ma Doon Road cuts over and down, we could see the flame-topped chimneys of Grangemouth and, to the west, Glasgow and perhaps Arran on a clear day, and north to the

Trossachs. The main arteries through the town are the Glasgow Road, heading west, which at 'the foot of the town' morphs into the Stirling Road, heading east. Now, it feels like Kilsyth was always a place to be going from, to somewhere else, but back then it was the centre of our lives. References were local too. 'Awa' tae Denny', a village about five miles east, was what my gran used to say when really she meant GTF. If folk weren't going away anywhere on holiday and staying at home for the summer, they'd say they were going to 'Twechar Beach' – Twechar being the resolutely landlocked former mining village a couple of miles west.

With other kids from the nearby houses, I'd go up to the Big Stane to play, or to the Couches beyond, and occasionally, though we weren't allowed, over them to an abandoned, flooded quarry carved out of the hill that, at that time, had a huge, unprotected drop to the water below. Sometimes we'd go further, down to the Welfare with its swing park, red blaes tennis courts and a football pitch that would take the skin off your knees in an instant, trampolines and putting green. We'd all go out on our bikes in that '70s way that, when we talk now to others the same age, wonder how we were allowed out just to roam, to play, to go over the hills or up the glen or around the dam and nobody quite knew where we were but we'd always be back in time for our tea.

Kilsyth is just another wee Scottish town, a satellite to Glasgow that's now more of a commuter town than it used to be. The Pipe Band still leads a march through the streets in the early hours of Hogmanay every year to 'see out the auld year', a custom dating from 1838. It's a place I couldn't wait to get out of, and I left for university in Edinburgh when I was eighteen. Because of family, it's a town I return to regularly, and I go for the same walks that I used to when I was a child and a teenager. It's the kind of town where, when my first book came out, someone mentioned it on the town's Facebook page and a school friend posted a photograph of me in double denim and a flat-top from my days at Kilsyth Academy, and my cousin saw it and emailed it to me. It's the kind of town that has its problems and issues, of course, but also laughs and says, don't forget where you're from.

When I'm there now I'm amazed at how close to the countryside it is. How I can watch the weather come in over the Campsie Fells, the hills to the west of the Kilsyth Hills, and see the planes fly overhead as they come in to land at Glasgow Airport if the wind's coming in from the west, and the skeins of geese arriving at the change of season.

From where I write, I can see, above the Scots pinewoods of Abernethy, a distant ridge. I can watch the weather coming in, and the hill will sometimes mist up with the grey sheen of rain and disappear in the way the Campsies would also disappear when rain was coming. This too makes me feel at home.

FOR YEARS NOW I HAVE been making *walkDrawings* – where I record the walks and routes I take using a handheld GPS. They're mainly around Abernethy, though I have walks from all kinds of places, including repeated ones around St Ninian's Isle on Shetland.

They started as part of the process of making *dead amongst the living* – the artwork I created about dead trees. I needed to find a way to retrace my steps and return to the snags I was looking for. They were often difficult to find a second, third, fourth time, as I wasn't looking for them in any systematic way, as I might if doing it 'properly', using transects as an ecologist would. In looking for these snags, it was easy to get lost or disoriented and, even in such a small area, to forget where one tree was in relation to another. Sometimes, depending on the light, they seemed so obvious; at other times they disappeared completely. On a dreich day, it was impossible, from amongst the trees, to say where the north or the south was. After a while, I started using a GPS to map these walks – setting off from the house where I was staying and creating waypoints where I'd found the trees and mapping where I walked. These drawings show my leavings and returns back to the house, and the same and different paths I would walk depending on what I saw and what I would aim for.

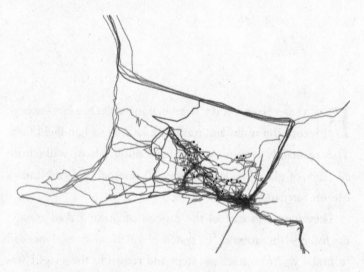

At one point I placed 10cm² steel plates at the north side of each snag I found – around thirty in all. I'd partially coated each with an acid-resistant (and so water-resistant) ground, leaving a circle of exposed metal in the middle. I wanted to gather some sense of place, some weathering, some physical evidence of time passing. I left them exposed to the elements for two months so the moisture would rust the metal that remained exposed. When I retrieved the plates, they were marked where rain, snow, frost, damp or dew had touched the metal.

Later, I did the same with bigger steel plates (36cm²), asking a friend to leave each plate in the forest for a month at a time, over the space of a year. Each month's plate was slightly different; some were more rusted from months that had had more rain or had been damper or dewier. Some had echoes of where birch leaves or pine needles had fallen and lain on the plates. May's plate was stained blue where pollen had interacted with moisture and the metal. The plates became compelling objects in themselves, as well as the matrix for the prints I made running them through the etching press, where the rust marks transferred onto paper.

When I started volunteering with the Royal Society for the Protection of Birds (RSPB) on the Abernethy reserve, walking with rangers, foresters and ecologists as they were doing their work, I used my GPS to map these walks too. They showed not just where we'd been, but how particular activities dictated how we moved through and across the land.

I liked the traces, their marks, how they worked like a pencil line on a page. Paul Klee's observation that 'drawing is taking a line for a walk' and Richard Long's work *A Line Made by Walking* – where he walked back and forth in a straight line across a piece of grass until it was worn with the indentation of his repeated steps – writ large. I started to remove the maps and contours to be left just with the lines.

We were often involved in the maintenance of the reserve. Sometimes we walked erratically along paths and tracks, moving from one side to the other clearing any trees within two metres to ensure that the paths would remain free of fallen branches, should there be a heavy snowfall.

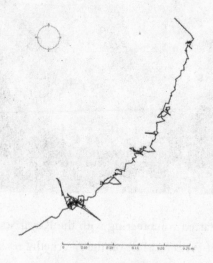

I once followed an ecologist who was counting the regeneration of Scots pines. This involved walking transects: straight lines plotted across the landscape at equal distances apart that allow representative estimates of, in this case, Scots pine regeneration. In the drawing made, shown in the photograph of the etching below, I can see the lines of each transect walked: parallel, equally spaced, east to west. I can see the curve of the track we walked up to get to the start of the survey transects, the straight lines walked, and how we got back to the car. I can also see where, boots off, we took a detour in order to cross a river at a narrower point to get to another, longer transect. A record of a day's walking doesn't reveal the labour, the conversations, changes in weather and changes in light, what was learnt and what was seen, nor the *hillworn*-ness at the end of the day. It doesn't tell us that we finished and walked back to the car in near darkness, and what it felt like to not quite know where I was, almost, until the car came into view.

The straightness of line belies the lay of the land, and I remember how, for each of these long transects, we walked in silence and in single file, noting any new growth, gauging the age of each young tree. The world became smaller and more immediate, to the line and footfall of the person in front, with a need for constant attention to the detail of what one was looking for. With that concentration other elements of place faded into the background. Only at the end of each transect did we stop and look up, at which point the whole of the place would come into view again.

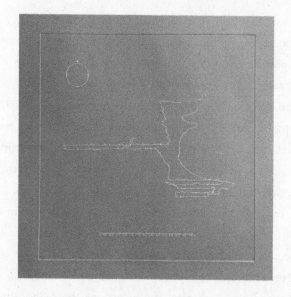

I turned my first few *walkDrawings* into etchings, and they became delicate lines in white ink on a beautiful grey 250g mould-made printmaking paper called Somerset Newsprint. I used a photopolymer plate – a technique that combines the essence of etching but uses light rather than acid to 'etch' a light-sensitive plate, creating a deep incision so the ink pushed into it forms a ridged surface on the paper when the plate with paper is run through the press.

The results are delicate, minimal imprints of thin lines on paper, lines that lose their meaning in terms of time and place, even memory, but gain something else, and the lines are thicker with repeated visits and time spent, and thin when only passing through.

THE FIRST TIME I CAME to Abernethy was to see the ospreys at Loch Garten. It's a place that has always, somehow, felt familiar to me, and I've no idea why. I can't imagine ever not having known it, though for most of my life I haven't.

I've spent early mornings on the shores of Loch Garten hearing the sound of geese calling from within a low-level morning mist that hides then softens the rise of the hills behind, and I've seen the first swallows arriving back: 27th April one year, 28th the next. Brown hares become visible in the fields each spring, though the numbers of footprints in the snow attest to their year-round residency. Red and roe deer appear at any time of the year, but in the long summer gloamings emerge miraculously and graze as night falls. Woodcock rode every evening, bats flick around the house, and moths tap against the windows. There are the Scots pines, of course, but amongst them are the tight tangles of juniper and the occasional flash of white birch bark or the red of rowan berries; lichen hangs like hair from branches, and bracken grows to more than a metre high by the time autumn comes. In summer, ospreys are often simply distant specks and swifts screech above the trees, sometimes so fast they are gone before you see them.

I've taken countless walks through the forest and along the tracks towards Ryvoan bothy and An Lochan Uaine to the forests of Glenmore and to Loch Morlich, with Meall a' Bhuachaille on one side, and Bynack Beg and Bynack More on the other. Sometimes, if I stop for breath, midges swarm thick and rampant around me like the cloud of dust that surrounds Pigpen in the *Peanuts* cartoons.

I love the changes of rhythm and the motions here: the scud of clouds on a windy afternoon that makes hills and valleys seem to undulate. The changing light. From the edges of the forest and looking onto moors and the mountains beyond, trees which usually blend into the background become spotlit by a late, low afternoon sun; a small birch in a gully on a distant hillside suddenly springs out in autumn with its silver bark and yellowing leaves.

It's a storied place, but a lived-in, everyday place, and I've come to know it through visits, then house-sitting, research for my doctorate, volunteering with the RSPB and now by living here.

Abernethy is the largest area of ancient, remnant Caledonian pinewoods left in Scotland and, at last count, around 5,000 species have a home here. A total of 20% of these are considered nationally rare or endangered,[16] and its multiple conservation statuses attest to its importance. In its habitats and microhabitats rare hoverflies, lichens and flowers can be found, and red squirrels, crested tits, crossbills, pine martens, wildcats and a significant proportion of the UK's capercaillie population – over 80% – is found in Strathspey.[17] In fact, to call it just a forest does a disservice to the complexities of what lies within it. Ron Summers' encyclopaedic *Abernethy Forest*[18] delves into its complex histories and myriad ecologies in ways that, as a layperson, I can only touch on. I write this place as I've come to know it, as a visitor, and now, as someone who stays here.

Throughout Abernethy, in the forest and on its fringes and hinterlands, you'll find evidence of past presence and activity, if you know where to look and what to look for, and it's a delight to come across such things. In one part of the forest lies the faint trace of the line of an old railway track (a Puggy line) built to transport wood out of the forest during the First World War by the Canadian Forest Corps who were stationed here. From earlier periods there's evidence of dams, lime and corn kilns, sheilings and saw pits where the wood was taken and sawn by hand. Prehistoric flints have also been found.[19]

I've seen an old pine tree, dated to the seventeenth century, and on its damaged trunk splinters have been hewn to make fir candles – strips of resin-saturated wood that were dried and used as lights. A rough 'B' is carved into the trunk. In 1763, a letter was written on behalf of James Grant, the owner of Abernethy at that time, to his head forester: 'A most pernicious Custom has prevail'd of cuting Pieces from the body of Large and thriving Trees for Candles and other Uses, which Wood for Candles has been even sold and sent out of the Estate of

Strathspey.'[20] Grant's head forester further reported, 'Whereas the very greatest Abuses of every kind have been committed in all the Woods of Strathspey belonging to the Family of Grant, stealing, cuting, barking and otherways destroying them, and by raising Moorburn in the adjacent parts, to such a degree, that if some effectual Remedies are not provided against such destructive Practices in time coming, these Woods must in a short time be entirely ruined and lost'.[21] Steven and Carlisle note that 'In 1722 the penalty for stealing timber was a fine of £10 Scots for a first offence, rising to £40 Scots for the third, and any subsequent offence rendered the offender liable to hanging.'[22]

While the seventeenth century saw some timber removal, it was really in the early eighteenth century that the industry took off. It carried on through to the mid-nineteenth century, which saw sawmills constructed and foundries built. In an area of moorland, a ranger once showed me remnants of a dam wall at the end of a flat, raised valley floor surrounded by a gentle slope where trees once stood. The lower end was blocked off, creating an artificial dam that flooded, and the trees around its edges were felled and floated down the dam, to a burn, to the River Nethy, and then to the Spey and onwards to the sea. There were water-driven sawmills throughout Strathspey, and, for a short spell, boring mills, including one at Dell in Nethy Bridge which made wooden water pipes by coring the trunks of pine trees. With grand ideas to float the pipes down the Spey to Garmouth, and then ship them by boat to markets in London, this proved uneconomical and the enterprise was short-lived.[23] In the visitor information room in the Nethy Bridge Community Centre they've a section of one of the pipes, and it really is quite a beautiful thing.

Steven and Carlisle note that in 1839 there were still around ninety men working in forestry in Abernethy, earning around £7 per year, but as the nineteenth century progressed, timber made way for 'sport'. I read the historian T. C. Smout describing how 'the end of active forestry in 1878 resulted in the clearance of at least 104 people to make a deer reserve that employed five.'[24]

One of my favourite walks takes me through the forest and up a track to a view of the Cairngorms beyond, and to where the tumbled-down walls of abandoned settlement buildings are still obvious, and around which you can still see the corrugated patterns of their field systems.

Humans and ownership and politics and class divisions have shaped this forest, but so too have natural forces: rain, winds, fire. The 'muckle spate' of 1829 caused flooding that affected vast areas of Strathspey and the North East.[25] F. H. Groome describes the River Nethy, which flows through the forest: 'A brook in drought, it is subject to violent spates, the greatest on record being those of 1829 and June 1880, when it flooded great part[s] of Nethybridge village, and changed all the level below into a lake.'

Fires have shaped this place as well. There was a big blaze in 1746, and in *In the Shadow of Cairngorm*, written in 1900, the Reverend W. Forsyth wrote about another later that century:

Another great fire is referred to by Sir Walter Scott (in a letter to Lord Montagu, 23rd June 1822), when the Laird of Grant is said to have sent out the *Fiery Cross* for help. Five hundred men assembled, 'who could only stop the conflagration by cutting a gap of 500 yards in width betwixt the burning wood and the rest of the forest. This occurred about 1770, and must have been a tremendous scene'.[26]

Jamieson's *Dictionary of the Scots Language* defines the Fiery Cross (or the fyre cross, as he calls it) as 'the signal sent from place to place, as expressive of the summons given by a chief or sovereign, to his vassals or subjects, to repair in arms, within a limited time, to the place of rendezvous appointed'.

Where the forest spills and thins out onto the hinterlands of the Cairngorms, on an area of heather moorland peppered by occasional granny pines that some folk call the savannah, I've seen black grouse, golden and sea eagles and, a couple of times, merlins too. Higher up, I've seen ring ouzels, golden plovers, dotterels and ptarmigan. Naturally regenerated younger trees have had the chance to grow now that deer numbers have been reduced – and by this I mean culled. It's also punctuated by snags, and a ranger once gave me another name for them – *kelo* – a Finnish term for a tree that has died, been dried out by winds and remains standing, often for centuries, only imperceptibly decaying. Some stand on the edges of secret lochans that lap against a variety of different types of shores, unseen from the paths, and burns occasionally become small waterfalls before they join the River Nethy.

There are all kinds of histories always there, of course, but ordinarily it's the here and the now that holds me: the *pruuk* of a raven somewhere above; the distant sound of a Search and Rescue helicopter high over the mountains or flying back to base; the shifting, changing forest itself. There's a long-term initiative to restore native trees out on the moorlands where they formerly grew, before they were felled for timber, before the place became over-grazed. Initially, much of this will be done through planting saplings, and eventually it's hoped that all regeneration will be natural. This restoration plan will take some species upwards to what would have been their natural limits, including to high-altitude, montane habitats. The time-scale for this is over the next 200 years,[27] and I like how we can be hopeful for timespans that are beyond our lifetimes. It can be hard to imagine what this place was like before and it can take all our imagination to consider what this place might become. I think of the artist Katie Paterson's work *Future Library*, where, in 2014, she planted 1,000 trees in an area just outside Oslo in Norway. These will supply the paper that will be used to produce an anthology of writing to be published in 2114. Each year, a writer will contribute a text – Margaret Atwood was the first to do so – and the work will be held in a trust and sit unpublished until 2114. We've a Future Library certificate – a foil block print – that hangs on our wall. The money raised from the prints supports the care of the forest and allows us one copy of the anthology when it's printed, but it's not something we'll ever see, and, not having children, I wonder where our copy will end up. It makes me consider how we might think beyond ourselves, about the importance of that hope inherent in what we leave for future generations.

In Abernethy the sense of gradual discovery never leaves you, and you never quite know what you might hear or see or find. I walk these forests on my own and with friends, and when I've volunteered I've helped with mending fences, filling in potholes, weeding, planting seedlings, brood counting and creating deadwood. Each activity brought me to different parts of this forest at different times of day, seasons, weathers. Lots of people have taught me all kinds of things about this place, but I've still so much to learn. There are people who have been here for so long the place is in their bones in ways I can only imagine.

Sometimes I take photos of unfamiliar lichens that hang from branches or in the neuks of fallen logs that I'll look up later, and I'll learn that some of the lichens are from families named *usnea* and *cladonia*, and that many lichens are important indicators of good air quality, and that over 220 different species of lichen have been found on Scots pine trees. But I've a memory like a sieve, and while I can hold the names of most birds and some flowers, lichens and grasses are beyond me. I think that it may be enough just to recognise witch's hair, horsehair and maybe pixie cups. The briefly familiar becomes unfamiliar or forgotten once more, to be rediscovered again the next time.

| *to speir* | to ask |
| *speirins* | inquiry; interrogation; investigation, used with the addition of different prepositions, as, *after, at* and *of* |

WHEN I WAS GOING THROUGH nineteenth-century Scots language dictionaries to compile *A Scots Dictionary of Nature*, a few of the words I found pulled me back to my family in that way that language can pull us back to different times and places. Being in a *dwam*. Going for a *dauner*. My papa pointing out the *speugs* that would flock to eat the stale bread we'd thrown out onto the back green. My mum will still say someone is *speirin'* if they're digging for information, and I'll still be *scunnered* if I'm fed up. When I looked through these old dictionaries I was drawn to the unfamiliarity of their words and the lusciousness of the descriptions that often accompanied their definitions. I gathered together words that originated from all over the country – some were probably very local, some more widespread, and I didn't distinguish them by place or by origin; I simply loved their possibilities and the images they conjured up. *Havoc burds, those large flocks of small birds which fly about the fields after harvest; they are of different species, though all of the linnet tribe.* Some of the words may have been used by my ancestors, although probably most were not, and would have been as strange to them as they are to me. It was the feeling of how they rolled around my mouth, and how evocative they were that made them stick in my mind: *tyning, the act of losing; the state of being lost.*

I was drawn to the words that made me pause and pay attention to familiar things described in unfamiliar ways and how we might connect them. Some, when gathered together, revealed nuances that have been lost in the speed and discon-nection of today. Gathering and list-making is something that I have continued to do. By gathering words, then playing with their order, I see how they can come together to reveal other meanings.

twalmonth a year

crap o' the water	the first water taken from a well after midnight on 31st December, said to bring luck for the new year
merry-meetings	New Year's Day merrymakings
handsel-e'en	the eve of the first Monday of the new year. (*handsel,* a gift bestowed to commemorate an inaugural occasion, event or season, for example, the beginning of the year, the first visit to a friend's new home or the commencement of a new undertaking, the wearing of new clothes, and so on, with the idea of bringing good luck to the recipient)
handsel Monday	the first Monday of the new year
gaun-days	the last fortnight of January and the first of February
lang-war-days	the month of March
craw-Sunday	the first Sunday in March, on which crows begin to build nests

Saint Causlan's flaw	a shower of snow in March
warlock-fecket	a magic jacket woven from the skins of water snakes at certain periods of a March moon
outcome	that season in which the days begin to lengthen
tuquheit storm	a designation given to the storm which almost invariably occurs in the month of March, and which is conjoined, in the traditionary observations of the peasantry, with the reappearance of the lapwing from its retreat during winter
ware-time	the season of spring
foreyear	the earlier part of the year, as the spring
aitseed	oat sowing and its season
bar-seed	the time of sowing bear-seed
bear-seed	barley; the time of sowing barley or of preparing the ground for it
March-moon	in the increase of the March Moon, the Highlanders cut withes of the woodbine that clings about the oak. These they twist into a wreath or circle, and carefully preserve it till the next March; and when children are troubled with hectic fevers, or when any one is consumptive, they make them pass through this circle thrice, by putting it over their heads, and conveying it down about their bodies

borrowing days	the last three days of March. These days being generally stormy, our fore-fathers have endeavoured to account for this circumstance by pretending that March borrowed them from April, that he might extend his power so much longer. Those who are much addicted to superstition will neither borrow nor lend on any of these days, lest the articles borrowed should be employed for the purposes of witchcraft against the lenders
hunt-the-gowk	a fool's errand, especially applied to one on which a person is sent on the first day of April
witch-Sabbath	a gathering of all the witches in Scotland on the evening between the first Friday and Saturday in April
gab	the last days of April, anticipating the weather of May
gowk-storm	a storm consisting of several days of tempestuous weather, the end of April or the beginning of May, when the *gowk*, or cuckoo, visits
reid day	the third day of May
May-bird	the whimbrel, a person born in May (proverb: '*May birds are aye wanton*')
May-gobs	cold weather in the second week of May

Beltane	depending on where you are in Scotland, a festival formerly kept by herds and young people on 1st May and 21st June
Barchan's Day	21st June
worm-month	the month of July
Bulgan's Day	4th July, the feast of St Martin
Lammas	the beginning of August
Lammas-flood	heavy rain and floods about 'Lammas'
Lammas-stream	a strong and high spring-tide in August
Lawrencemas	23rd August
reid day	a day in September before which wheat is generally sown. On *reid-een*, or the eve of this day, the hart and the hind are believed to meet for copulation
neep-seed	turnip seed, the time for sowing turnip seed
brak-back, *break-back*	the harvest moon as entailing heavy labour
stooky-Sunday	the Sunday in harvest on which the greatest number of stooks [haystacks] is seen in the fields
hin-hairst, *hint o' hairst*	the end of harvest; the time between harvest and winter
go-harvest, *goe-hairst, -harst*	the fall, when the season declines, or is about to go away; including the time from the ingathering of the crop till the commencement of winter
lang halter time	the season of the year when, the fields being cleared, travellers and others claimed a common right of occasional passage

go o' the year	the latter part of the year, when the day goes very short
backend	the close of a season or of the year; autumn, winter
huntsman's moon	the October moon
winter-Saturday	the last Saturday of October on which the winter half-year begins
winter-Sunday	the last Sunday of October
back-end o' the year	the latter part of the year
Hallowmas	the season of All-hallows; the first week of November
Andyr's-day	the day dedicated to St Andrew, the Patron Saint of Scotland, 30th November
howe o' the year	the winter solstice
how o' winter	the middle or depth of winter, from November to January
reid day	7th December
dede time o' the year	midwinter, when there is no vegetation
daft-days	the holidays at Christmas and the New Year
singing-e'en	the last night of the year, Hogmanay
hogmanay	31st December
Carlin's e'en	the last night of the year
water-custom	the custom of going to a well near midnight on 31st December to draw the first water of the new year; supposed to bring good luck for the year ahead

ox-e'en titmice

O NE SUMMER, EVERY MORNING I'D have breakfast at the kitchen table and look out over the trees – birches, mainly, before the swathes of Scots pines. Coal tits, blue tits, chaffinches and occasional siskins would fly in from the trees and a blackthorn hedge to feed from the nyjer seeds that filled a little metal cup on the windowsill. So small and fleeting in the bigger landscape that was behind them, it took me ages to think to film them, to frame them in a way that they'd become front and centre, with their hurried breathing, the droplets of water on their breasts, their rapid wingbeats and incessant movement. These tiny birds. Coal tits weigh on average 8 to 10 grams, and later, when I walked with a bird ringer and saw how he held these birds in his hand, I saw how delicate they were, how easily they could be broken.

UNLIKE ABERNETHY — WHERE THE trees peter out into the higher reaches of moorland, and where straggled remnants of its bigger, former reach remain — the Moray forest of Culbin, about an hour's drive north and slightly east from the northernmost point of Abernethy, has definite edges. To its northwest edge, the horizontal plane of the sea to shore is sharply abutted by the verticality of the trees; when closer, you'll see it's occasionally softened by broom and whin, but from a distance it's a stark right angle that defines the space of tree to shoreline on one side, fields to trees on the others.

Culbin Forest sits near the town of Forres. Its northward side hugs the Moray coastline and stretches eastward from Findhorn Bay to Nairn. Crows agitate on its defined edges, flying up from the surrounding farmland and into its trees. Culbin is a forest I've walked and cycled through many times, on my own and with friends, looking for birds and flowers. Compared to Abernethy, it is, relatively speaking, new — around 100 years old — though, in the way of growth and senescence, some of the trees in both Culbin and Abernethy will be of comparable ages, and like Culbin, Abernethy has large areas of plantation pines. Sometimes you can see older, gnarled grannies within, disrupting the straight uniformity of the planted trees.

Culbin has been, from the start, a planned forest, a constructed place. It was planted by the Forestry Commission in an area that was for centuries a stretch of sand dunes which ran for six miles along the coast, more than two miles wide in parts, which sometimes cast up massive sandstorms threatening the surrounding, rich farmland. Locals used the marram grass for thatch, and that further destabilised the dunes. A huge sandstorm in 1694 (or more likely 'a succession of gales of unprecedented strength') is said to have finally inundated and engulfed the estate, causing the River Findhorn to change course as well. It is said the remains of crofts and buildings still lie under what's now the forest.[28] Walking through it today, it seems remarkable that in the 1930s J. A. Steers could write of the impact of the trees on this landscape that 'the physiographer cannot help regretting that the nearest approach to a desert in the British isles is rapidly disappearing'.[29]

I love Culbin for its flatness and its uniformity and its difference. It's big enough to disorientate and confuse, though the first few times I was there, I didn't give it that respect. The trees feel uniform, at least at first, and the land is relatively contour-line free. I've sometimes felt lost, even if I wasn't really, like when I've strayed off-path to follow an unfamiliar bird call. Once I spent hours walking this forest, randomly choosing forks on the tracks and going onto smaller paths, thinking I knew roughly where I was going. I usually think I've a reasonably good sense of direction, and though I thought I knew where I was and that, if I kept going, maybe even just another mile, I'd get back to the car park, I had a wave of disquiet and uncertainty so strong that I turned and turned again, retracing my route, taking hours longer than I had intended, but surer about my place.

Plans for this forest show both its past and its future. They show what trees have been planted where and when. They show the different species – lodgepole, Scots and Corsican pines and Douglas firs. Future plans show felling and replanting schedules. Now, non-native species are likely to be replaced by native species like Scots pines and native broadleaves. In the design plan replicated below we can see the decades in which each part of the forest was planted, and other plans show which species are planted where.[30]

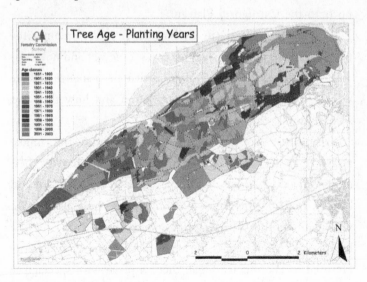

Such plans and maps are so seductive, with their clean lines, their determination, and though we can't see its colour-codedness here, we can still make out the careful delineations and compart-mentalisations, its very map-ness. I have a British Geological Survey map that defines land not by height and contours, but what is underneath the soil. It tells me that at this very moment I'm sitting on top of *psammite with thin quartzite subordinate semi-pelite and rare calcsilicate ribs*. I love the idea of resting on a rib.[31]

On maps the information is carefully gathered and organised, readable in the abstract, at least to some. But once I'm in the forest or on the hill I'm faced with the messiness of living, of growth and decay, the vagaries of the weather and how it shifts perceptions, and I love that more. It's the difference between looking at the *OS Explorer OL 57 Cairn Gorm and Aviemore*, and reading Nan Shepherd's *The Living Mountain*, and walking up onto the Cairngorm Plateau.

As with most forests, in Culbin, when you're amongst the trees, what's beyond the edges becomes irrelevant and unknow-able, and there's the sense of perpetual permanence despite what we know of cycles of regeneration and how they age, seed, regrow.

I've heard a forester talk about trees as crops. But, unlike a farmer, rather than annually, the forester will harvest their crops only every forty or fifty years, or longer. Human and beyond-human timescales intermingle in these places. We walked in another Moray forest and he showed me trees he had planted when he first started in the Forestry Commission. He used to take his tea break there, a place with spectacular views over to Culbin and beyond to the Moray Firth, until the trees grew so tall that he could no longer see beyond. Now, the trees were nearly ready to be felled, and he was soon to retire.

Standing near its edges on Culbin's seaward side, it's sometimes impossible to tell if what you can hear is a breeze through the branches or the sea on the shore. Surrounded by the trees, you might not realise how in places the firth still nips at and unpicks the northern seaward edges, or how young this forest actually is.

It's hard to imagine the volume of labour used to plant it, and how the shifting sands, wind and weather must have thwarted and frustrated even the most patient worker. The Forestry Commission planted young trees – Scots, Corsican and lodgepole pines – figuring out, as the years went on, which trees grew best where: 'The Corsican pine has been found the most suitable for the less fixed dunes; Scots pine thrives well on shingle and stable sand areas; and the lodgepole pine grows almost anywhere.'[32]

In earlier years when the forest was thinned, felled trees were used for pit props. Since the sand tended to be blown eastward, they worked west to east using a method known as 'thatching', which involved laying down and pegging brushwood (usually locally growing birch and broom) on the dunes to help fix the sand.

This method of planting had other, perhaps unforeseen but significant, consequences. Some of the brushwood may well have brought in species from elsewhere, kicking off Culbin's diverse ecosystem. And other species would have been carried in too, by birds or on the wind.

Different times of planting and distinct species are often obvious in the differing heights and subtle colour shifts in various sections of forest. You can see where the smooth grey bark of a stand of lodgepoles makes way for the rough reddening trunks of Scots pines. Occasional birch copses and rowan trees appear too, unplanned, but these pioneer species take their chances. An oak seedling grows, perhaps from an acorn brought in and dropped by a passing jay. Still, differences which might appear as orange next to pink on a map (or dark to medium grey!) are less obvious once in the midst of it, and irrelevant in the scheme of things. Size is deceptive too. In this forest the trees have found root in inhospitable soils, sand and shingle. Trees which have been growing for eighty years can have the girth and height of trees decades younger, grown in more fertile settings – such is the paucity of nutrients in places. Yet the poverty of this soil brings unexpected riches, for here, on top of the shingle beds, rare lichens carpet the ground and grow in the liminal spaces between one stand of trees and another.

Mary McCallum-Webster (1906–1985), a self-taught botanist, assiduously documented the flora of Moray. Culbin was one of her go-to places, and she wrote: 'The Culbin Forest can boast (but this is exceptional) over 550 species of plants. This includes the flora of the dune areas but not the mosses and lichens. Fungi are abundant and in mid-September even the amateur can add over 100 species between the edge of the forest and the sea.'[33] You can feel her love of Culbin in the care and attention with which she writes about it, and sense how her knowledge came from walking this forest again and again and again.

I've seen a fraction of the numbers of plants McCallum-Webster found here, and the lichens remain unknown to and unnameable by me, but that's all right. While I don't know Culbin like she did, or those who forest it do, I've come to know it better than I did, and knowing Culbin has helped me to know Abernethy more too. I've heard whitethroats in these woods and crested tits and crossbills. On the forest floor, I've seen pine cones gnawed by red squirrels. Butterflies like the green hairstreak and the Scotch argus make their homes here. Once, I startled an osprey which had been perched on a low branch, and it flew off in front of me, a fish still in its talons. Plants like creeping ladies' tresses, a type of wild orchid, and McCallum-Webster's favourite flowers, the wintergreens, grow there, including the rare *Moneses uniflora*, the one-flowered wintergreen. Her ashes are scattered there, amongst a colony of them, and I can't help but think she'd have felt Culbin as a home. I've seen one-flowered wintergreens there, and it's one I long to come across in Abernethy. In *Flora of Moray, Nairn and East Inverness*, McCallum-Webster noted that they were to be found 'in several places in the pine woods of Loch Mallachie', but the records are from 1910. A more recent report suggests there are two populations in Abernethy. Two! In all this space. And whether they are still there, or where they might be is something else again. I hope to find them one day, and hope that there are more, unfound as yet.

In Culbin, for the most part, all its species live in tension or in harmony with the elements: a changing climate, a dynamic coastline and human interventions that will sometimes protect and sometimes destroy. There are six-spot burnet moths and speckled wood butterflies and all kinds of flora and fauna I've not yet come across or been knowledgeable enough to recognise, including the rare lichens. I've seen Brent geese in the narrow channel at the place known as The Gut just outside its Nairn-side edge, where the forest spills into marshland before the sea.

Culbin is a forest that surprises me, though it shouldn't, really. It is a place that's newly created (relatively speaking), strategic, planned, yet within it lies nature's messiness, voraciousness, unbiasedness too. Red squirrels, crested tits, pine martens, deer, otters, 130 species of lichen and 500 flowering plants have all found a home, and I can't help but wonder how this landscape has changed and what's here now compared to one hundred years ago, and what the next hundred years will bring.

THE HAGGS IS A VILLAGE I often drive past, usually when heading up north from or down south to Glasgow. It's about five miles east of Kilsyth, and was the childhood home of my gran, where her two brothers and sister stayed until they died. I have often speculated about the origins of the name. Variously, in old Scots, 'haggs' can mean *wild, broken ground,* or *a piece of soft bog in a moor,* or *a hole in a moss from which peats have been cut,* or *a water-hollow, wet in winter and dry in summer* or *an islet of grass in the midst of a bog.* Recently, when I was trying to find out more about my gran's family's house, I came across a lecture given by the Reverend David Keir of Dennyloanhead Free Church in 1921, entitled 'Then and Now, Dennyloanhead, Bonnybridge and Haggs – Past and Present', where he clarifies that 'the name of Haggs suggests the nature of the district in former times. Hag means *a pit in mossy ground.'*

Map of Haggs, 1898.

When I drive to Glasgow from Strathspey, I take the A9 south and end up on the M80. If I'm cutting off to Kilsyth to visit my mum, I'll take the Haggs exit at Junction 7 and when I come off, I take a right at the mini-roundabout onto the A803.

Just beyond it, and into the left, at the bottom of a small cul-de-sac, I can still see the shed that used to be my Uncle Bobby's, and behind it, the back of the council house where my gran's family moved in the 1940s and where Aunt Mary and Uncles Tom and Bobby stayed until they died.

Between the shed and the house is the garden, where my Aunt Mary apparently set fire to a number of the letters and papers and birth certificates and family photographs she was the keeper of, after my uncles' deaths. '*That's what they did with old papers and correspondences*', my mum tells me regretfully. Before moving there, my gran's family stayed in a row of miners' houses that we think were condemned then demolished, and that's why they moved to Castleview Terrace, a council house on the other side of where the motorway now cuts. The entry in Groome's *Gazetteer of Scotland* tells us about the village as it was in the late nineteenth century.

> Haggs, a village and a *quoad sacra* parish in Denny parish, SE Stirlingshire. The village ¾ mile N by E of Castlecary station and 3⅛ miles SSW of Denny town, includes Hollandbush and is conjoint with Longcroft, Parkfoot and Dennyloanhead villages, extending 1½ miles along the road from Kilsyth to Falkirk. It acquired in 1836 a neat row of collier cottages, terminating at one end in a large building, intended for a store. The *quoad sacra* parish, constituted in 1875, is in the presbytery of Stirling and synod of Perth and Stirling; the minister's stipend is £170. The church, erected as a chapel of ease in 1840, presents a handsome appearance. There is also a subscription school. In the neighbourhood of Hollandbush was fought, on the 15th of August 1645, the battle of Kilsyth. Pop. of village (1891) 623; of registration district and *q.s.* parish. (1891) 1560.— *Ord. Sur., sh. 31, 1867.*

Amongst some old paperwork my mum found a partial family history – not quite a family tree – typed up by one of her cousins. Fragmented snapshots of lives captured in short paragraphs and cherry-picked details that say a little but, really, not very much:

All my immediate aunts and uncles (Taylors) were born in 137 Kilsyth Road, Haggs (a room and kitchen). They also occupied 141 Kilsyth Road. No indoor water or toilet, a washhouse and toilet to the rear. Both accommodations were part of a miner row (terraced house being accommodation for mine workers). 137 being the gable end to the east.

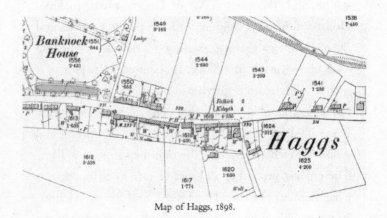

Map of Haggs, 1898.

Another of my mum's cousins, Jim (the son of my gran's oldest sister Liz and her husband Walter), says he remembers the two houses, and that the boys lived in one house and the girls in the other with their mother and father. According to the birth certificates, their father, William Taylor, was, variously, a foundry worker, a coal miner or a general labourer, depending on which of his children's birth certificates you look at. Their mother, variously named Jean, Jane or Jeannie, likely worked in service or stayed home.

We found a photograph of my gran at the back of the auld

hoose, which is how my mum and her cousin describe it. She's young, wearing a dark dress with a lace collar and buttons down the front that I imagine might be mother of pearl and which are slightly unevenly spaced, and flat Mary Jane shoes. I wonder what the occasion was and who took the photograph. She's standing by the fence, on dirt, not grass. She has an almost-smile, I think, and her hair is neatly parted at the side. Her eyes are dark and serious, as I remember them.

We don't know when my family moved into 137 and 141 Kilsyth Road. We reckon they took on one house and had to take on the second as the family expanded. It seems likely that my gran's parents were local to the area. I can't quite imagine the reality of what it was like to live there, at that time, or whether I only conjecture poverty and difficulty. I only hope that by the time they had moved in and started their family, conditions had improved from this report, 'Notes on Miners' Houses, Part VII', published in the *Glasgow Herald* on 30 January 1875:

A drive of four miles or so brings us to Haggs, a mining village, in which the houses are owned by Mr Wilson, of Banknock Colliery, and by persons living in the village. The Haggs, in various respects, is in a disgraceful state, and some of Mr Wilson's houses are much in need of repair. The old evil of dampness is present in almost every house I visited – damp in the beds, and in wet weather dripping from the ceiling, and being caught in a bowl. The back room of one of the houses was cold enough and damp enough to give one toothache in ten minutes. Stone floors are laid in the kitchen; wooden floors in the room. Farther, along the row are half a dozen houses belonging to other proprietors, one of them most objectionably situated – the floor being a couple of feet lower than the street in front and the garden ground behind. They are all damp and dark – so damp that three of the number are not tenanted. The houses here are rented at about £2 12s for single apartments and £3 10s for rooms and kitchens. The worst feature of Haggs, however, is the indescribably filthy condition of the back-yards. There are no ash pits, and the only closet I saw was so dirty that it could not be used. The result is that the kitchen gardens are poisoning the air, and are allowed to do so all the year through, no one providing for the refuse being removed. It is hard to guess what the local Authority for Haggs conceives to be the proper discharge of its duty. The water supply is also far from satisfactory, owing to neglect on the part of those who should interest themselves in the wants of the village. It is got from springs led into various pumps, and when procurable is of excellent quality. There are four of these pumps in the village, and I was told that all of them are at present out of repair, so that no water can be obtained. In these circumstances, the people go to the 'smiddy' near the pit, where there is a spring, and their wants are supplied, but in summer they are not allowed to take this water, which is reserved for cattle grazing in fields belonging to Mr Wilson. I asked several persona why the proprietor would not allow them to take the water in summer, and the first reply, 'Because he keeps't for his beese,' was the explanation given in every case, or at least the answers were of precisely similar import. The last resource is to go to Castlecary, where a farmer gives water on condition that he shall receive a day's work from the recipients during the season.

Just outside Haggs is the 'New Row'. The houses, which are of brick, are held from Mr Wilson, the single apartments being rented at 5s 6d a month, and the rooms and kitchens at £3 12s a year. The floors in the kitchen are of stone, the rooms being laid with wood. They are not bad houses, but the surroundings are ill kept. Ashes and other refuse are thrown in front of the houses although a large ash-pit is provided behind. One of the tenants told me it was not customary to lay the ashes down before the doors, but I fear it is too general. The only water available for the people in the New Row is that which is taken out of a burn down at Holland Bush, and the banks of which sufficiently indicate its quality. It was in flood when I saw it. A wine glassful which I get in one of the houses assumed a deeper brown on Nessler's mixture being added to it, showing that it was impure. The children, I was told, wade in it, and otherwise increase its pollution. In summer, when the burn is dry, the villagers have no water. 'What do you do then?' I asked. 'Weel, we get it frae a neebor's wall doon at the Bush, but he doesna' let us tak' it.' 'In short, you steal it?' 'Ay, we jist steal it, when we can. Then we catch rain water, which is better than the burn at ony time.'

In the digital archives of Falkirk District Council I found a photo of the miners' row.

One night, I sat with my mum talking and going through old photographs and documents she had stored in a plastic bag. Postcards from South Africa and Italy, where her uncles were stationed during the war, envelopes lined in black containing death notices of people we don't know. Birth and death certificates, frustratingly not everyone's, haphazardly gathered together and bound by elastic bands.

Memories and recollections of things not thought about in years. Little snippets sparked that reveal just that little bit more.

In her cousin's family history is a mention of a woman who my mum hadn't thought about for years, but now remembers from childhood.

'*Aye*', my mum says, '*Lizzy Anderson. I remember her very clearly saying to me, "Now, Jean, you'll just have to keep your eye on your mother, because she's had a very hard life of it." Because Granny Taylor kept her home and she did all the housework and washing for her brothers, who were grocers, bakers and miners.*'

'*Think of that,*' my mum says of the toil my gran would have to do for her brothers and sisters. '*No washing machine and a room and kitchen and that, and all the different kinds of clothes, there were no pit baths or anything. And, and I can't mind what arm, now, but did you ever notice that one arm was more developed than the other? It might have been the right arm. One was much thicker than the other, all that washing.*'

And now I want to go back and look at all the photographs of my gran, to see if one arm remained thicker than the other for the rest of her life.

simmering

aifer	the exhalations which arise from the ground on a warm, sunny day; hot, fierce, kindling
baumy	balmy
beek, beik	to bask in the sun
coldingham-packmen	cumulus clouds in the north or east on fine summer afternoons
dahie	warm, misty, 'muggy'
fire	sheet-lightning; the sultriness preceding a thunderstorm
fire-dairt	lightning
glorgie	sultry, applied to a warm suffocating day, with a darkened sun
hangall	a cold, damp, easterly wind blowing from the sea in summer
huam, houin	the moan of an owl in the warm days of summer
jock-startle-o'-stovie	the exhalations arising from the ground on a warm summer-day

king's-weather	the exhalations arising from the earth on a warm day
land-tide	the undulating motion of the air, seen on a hot day
leisom, leisome, liesome	warm; sultry
lunkie	close and sultry
mathy	warm and misty
meef, meeth, meith, moth	hot, sultry
meethness	sultriness; great heat
merry dancers	the Aurora Borealis; the exhalations from the earth in a warm day, as seen flickering in the atmosphere
muith	warm and misty
a muith morning	soft; calm; comfortable
muth	hot, sultry
ouder, owder	a light mist or haze, such as is sometimes seen at sunrise; the flickering exhalations from the ground, in the sunshine of a warm day
scowr	a slight shower; a passing summer shower
simmer	to bask; to enjoy the warmth and brightness of summer
simmer lift	the summer sky
sinny	sunny
smoor	a stuffy atmosphere
smurack	a slight summer shower

spiry	warm; parching
startle-o'-stovie	the exhalations seen to rise from the ground, with an undulating motion, in a warm sunny day
summer-blink	a transient gleam of sunshine
summer-cloks	sunbeams dancing in the atmosphere of a fine summer day
summer-couts	the exhalations seen to ascend from the ground in a warm day; the gnats which dance in clusters on a summer evening
summer-flaws	the quivering appearance of the atmosphere on a warm day; a swarm of gnats dancing in the air
summer-haar	a slight breeze from the east which often rises after the sun has passed the meridian
summer-sob	a summer storm
sweltry	sultry
tahie, tauchey, taughie	warm and moist
ure	a haze in the air; a coloured haze which sunbeams cause in summer; in passing through the air
warm-wise	rather warm, sultry
wildfire	summer lightning
yoam	to blow with a warm, close air
youther	a haze; flickering ground exhalations in heat

FROM THE MOMENT WE'RE BORN, our horizons and domains of familiarity gradually expand in ever-increasing circles. It starts with a pinprick, a mother to a pram, to a house, to family, to garden, to school, and then travels out and beyond and away and away. Our movements, our worlds, physical and psychic, expand exponentially from the smallest of locales and the earliest of times, though for some more than others. My mum thinks my papa went to Ireland once (where, why and with whom is unknown), but after he was married we couldn't think of a time he ever left Scotland. I think the furthest south my gran would have ventured was to visit her sister Martha in Huddersfield, and I only remember her doing that the once. I'm not sure that my gran and papa were ever anywhere as far north as I am now. Even during the war, my papa was with the War Department Constabulary, guarding the ordnance factory at Bishopton, just outside Glasgow, while my gran's brothers were in Italy and South Africa (and what must it have been like to travel to these places, after their lives before, and what must it have been like to return home after?). Contained lives, and they might have been fine with that.

The lockdowns for Covid-19 physically restricted me in a way I could barely have imagined, and the drive down the A9 to see my mum, to the other home I've always taken for granted, ceased. All non-essential journeys stopped. My GPS *walkDrawings* of that time are records of my local walks. They show me how my world became smaller in scope, but perhaps more deeply felt for that. They show paths and tracks that I walk with regularity, and occasional veers off-path into the woods in the hunt for birds or flowers. They criss-cross and repeat, but these are over days and weeks and months and years, and they are desire-lines of my own making, though sometimes I am following in others' footsteps and pathways. And from the pinprick of the house they etch deeper and deeper, and reach out and out and out.

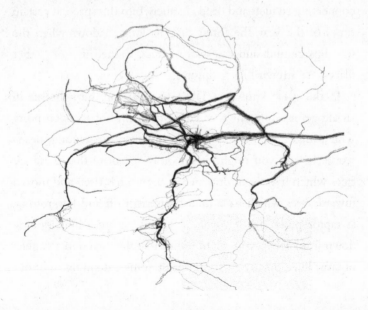

APPROACHING CULBIN FOREST FROM THE Nairn side, a larger liminal space wavers between sea and land, one in constant transition with light and shadow, salt and water, the sounds of the waves on one side, wind through the branches on the other. The land is punctuated by dark pools of water, connecting rivulets and deep channels. Into this space, at certain times of the year, the forest casts its long shadows when the sun dips behind, and carcasses of trees, washed in from other places, are strewn like sculptures.

In the space known as The Gut, trees spill into the sea in an altogether different way. Here stand lines of wooden posts, which might at first be fancifully mistaken for standing dead-wood. In fact you might erroneously speculate that these are trees which have been drowned as the sea has risen and moved inward, trees which have then been sawn off and left, rotting, as raptor posts. But if you look closely, or are a bird looking down from above, you might notice that they stand in a pattern of cross lines, northwest to southeast, some extending right out into the water. They've a different provenance, however: they are anti-glider posts, constructed to deter enemy landings during the Second World War.

They remind me of an artwork I went to visit once, *The Lightning Field*. It was made in the 1970s by Walter De Maria, a North American land artist. Situated on a high desert plain in Western New Mexico, De Maria's installation consists of a grid of 400 finely polished steel poles, two inches in diameter and averaging just over twenty feet in height, each needle-sharp at their tip, forming a grid exactly one mile by one kilometre in size. The poles are inserted into the ground in such a way that the tip of each pole is at exactly the same height above sea level. The sculpture can be viewed from a distance, but you can walk amongst the poles too, or around the peripheries. The work confounded me when I visited it: how it changed as the daylight changed, with the poles shifting from present to barely visible, from shafts of light when the sun hit them in certain ways to blackened in shadow. How the poles seemed to connect land to sky, and land and sky to weather, how the work attuned us to the weather, the possibility of rain, the direction of the wind and changes in temperature that might herald a storm – a storm that would bring the lightning to the field, and to us. I wonder about the process of appropriating the land for this work; no land is ever quite an empty space.

The Lightning Field demands effort and attention. You have to book well in advance in order to see it, and even the process of getting to the site once in New Mexico takes planning. You make your way to a small New Mexican town where you leave your car at the rendezvous point, then you are driven for about an hour and dropped off overnight at a small cabin, with supper and breakfast left for you. You're collected again the next day. It's a privileged position you find yourself in: only six people stay in the cabin at any one time, and every part of your journey alerts you to how special the place is, how attentive you have to be to this art, how important it is (or the artist or the artworld thinks it is), and even though I was sceptical, it did make an impact on me. My time and the space there sits as a contained and clear memory in my head, even as the journey to and from it has receded and blurred with other road trips, other times. Still, I think back to *The Lightning Field* and find it amazing that, for all my memories of the time I spent there, I can't recall any birds at all, just feelings of light and vastness and space.

At The Gut beside Culbin I am struck by some of the same feelings – how these posts staple land to sky, insinuating themselves into both. Unlike *The Lightning Field*, these posts are not polished steel, nor are they pin-point accurate in height: instead, they've rotted to a lesser or greater degree, and some have resisted weather and water better than others. Connecting sea and sky and solid to air, these remnants snag our eyes and call for some attention. At the base of some of these posts lie owl pellets, and they've become watchtowers for birds, perhaps now their only function.

I've seen Brent geese and wintering sea ducks, swifts and swallows, heard the sounds of willow warblers spilling into the liminal space between forest and shoreline from their perches on the trees, and, once, a merlin chasing a meadow pipit. I wonder what the forest of Culbin looked like at the time these glider posts were installed. What were the height of the trees, the views into and from within, the lengths of the shadows cast? Did the wood for them come from Culbin itself or someplace close?

We don't often have the luxury of a rich span of time spent in a place like *The Lightning Field*, with little distraction and a single focus. It's strange how being in a completely different place and circumstance took me back there. Perhaps that day in Culbin it was the light: how the sun spread over the mosses and grasses and reeds, shimmering them green and brown and gold, and how it struck the glider posts a bright silver-grey in contrast to the storm-deep purple-grey sky beyond.

The lockdowns also reminded me to pay attention to what it is to be in one place and stilled, to notice the shifts from spring to early summer, to new growth and changing colours – white anemones and wood sorrel to yellow tormentils and bird's-foot trefoil, the sky-blues of the speedwells; and, in midsummer, the way the sunlight hits the trees and shifts the shimmer of the birches from silver to sap, phthalo, helio, veridian greens, and when it rounds to the sky behind the birches at the burn in its evening light, the trunks and branches are revealed through the leaves like an X-ray of their bones.

warrachie rough and knotty,
as applied to a trunk of a tree

Heather and blaeberries and the scarlet of a cowberry. The flowers that hide among and between: cow-wheats and northern bedstraw, tormentil, early dog violet. A yellow flash of a siskin disrupts the still and the staccato drum of a woodpecker, the call of a cuckoo in the middle distance and a buzzard mewing overhead. Tree pipits fall in body and sound.

Just as the blaeberries become ripe for eating, the delicate stems of creeping ladies' tresses start to push through and upwards. And I want there to be a capercaillie just in the woods off to the edge of the path, but there is none.

SOMETIMES WHEN WALKING IN ABERNETHY I'll hear a chattering of finches overhead, and at other times, a sound like someone clicking two nails together. Perhaps a pine cone will fall near to where I've been standing, and when I look up, I'll see a movement, a flutter above, a bird or two hanging upside down on the cones.

Crossbills are a type of finch perfectly adapted to deal with the pinewoods. As the name suggests, its bill crosses at the tip, and this helps them prise open pine cones to remove their seeds. You'll sometimes hear them, then see a flash of brick-red or green. My association with them is entwined with being in Abernethy, although I've seen them in Culbin, the Trossachs and elsewhere in the Highlands. And, most remarkably for me, once, a pair on North Uist. Sometimes you'll see them perching on the topmost branches of the pines, though at other times they are more elusive and only an occasional, fleetingly noisy, passing presence.

Once, earlier in my time in Abernethy when I didn't know

it as well, I went for a walk, hoping to see some crossbills. I'd decided to walk to a lochan I'd seen on a map. I was wanting, but not expecting, to see a diver, and saw instead a solitary widgeon. It was at the very end of May and uncharacteristically hot, breezy and sunny. Thick clouds of pine pollen had just lifted and at one point swept towards and over me, leaving a thin yellow-green film on my arms, my sunglasses and binoculars. It was a long, solitary walk, hot, and I hadn't brought enough water. After a good few miles I crossed a burn before the track swept uphill, and a young deer I startled bounded away through the trees. I walked beyond the lochan to where the track came to a larger burn, and I had the option to ford it or continue on the track as it curved up a sharp right, following the burn bank for a bit. I stopped there and, too hot and far enough away for the day, turned back.

It was the same route I'd taken the previous winter in a 4WD truck with an RSPB ranger as he went deer stalking. We had driven up beyond the lochan and followed the track when it turned right and skirted its edge, climbing southwest. We'd forded the burn a little further up, heading up to an area of grouse moorland. That day, it had been icy with a bitter wind that had forced the snow into thick drifts in some places. My hands got cold in the way that when they heat up again they prickle and throb. It was the first and only time that I had ever seen someone shoot a deer, and I still can't get my head around it even now. I was unable to write about it at the time, and it's too long ago now to try.

For all the romance of Nan Shepherd's *unpath*, sometimes I

like the conviction of a path. Gaston Bachelard wrote: 'We do not have to be long in the woods to experience the always rather anxious expression of "going deeper and deeper" into a limitless world. Soon, if we do not know where we are going, we no longer know where we are.'[34] And while Rebecca Solnit eloquently celebrates the possibilities of lostness in *A Field Guide to Getting Lost*,[35] sometimes certainty and solidity bring their own rewards. Once, I went out walking with a forester who said that he felt at home in forests and did not like mountains or open spaces. He wondered if it was to do with his fifteen years in the army, when he was trained always to look for cover. He said that he'd never been, or felt, lost in woodlands, even those he visited for the first time. I am not like that at all, and yet mountains and open spaces, the very space of them, can be as unnerving to me as I sometimes find the forest.

On that May walk, it suited me to have trees on either side and a dusty track that enabled a steady pace and views forwards and back. I came across only one solitary male crossbill, and even then, only fleetingly. It perched briefly on the topmost branch of a Scots pine next to the track before it flew back into the forest and away. The sun was behind it so I only caught its silhouette and a flash of red as it flew.

I READ ONCE THAT ECOLOGICAL ISLANDS are not necessarily those islands that are surrounded by water; rather they are microhabitats of difference within other larger ecosystems and habitats. For example, the decaying wood of a snag contains microhabitats for saproxylic species and can form its own distinct habitats within. The tops of the Cairngorm mountains form an environment for montane species not found at lower altitudes. And of course some islands (I think of the Galapagos and Madagascar) have plants and species that aren't found elsewhere because of their very *islandness*. Even in Scotland, the Shetland Islands and St Kilda have their own wrens – both specific subspecies – and St Kilda's house mouse became extinct after its people left. I like the thought of these ecological islands all around us, these microhabitats that are often hiding in plain sight, with whatever's within them doing their own thing.

corvid   (genus) a bird of the crow family (Corvidae)

corbie, corby   the raven. This, like the pyat or magpie,
                as well as the harmless crow, is, in the
                estimation of the vulgar and
                superstitious, a bird of evil omen.

I F I LEAVE KILSYTH BY driving up the Tak Ma Doon Road
over the hills to Carronbridge and turn west, I pass the Carron
Valley reservoir, where in the summer you might see an osprey.
I go through Fintry and Blanefield and cut back down on the
road that goes south, around the west side of the Campsie Fells
to Lennoxtown, before heading back through Torrance and
Milton of Campsie to Kilsyth. This road down to Lennoxtown
is the B822 and is known as the Crow Road, and sometimes
rooks will fly over. The phrase 'to take the Crow Road' comes
into my head, and I've heard some use the phrase to mean *take
the most direct route* and others use it to mean *to die.*

Another day, further north, I'm on the A9, the main artery from the Central Belt into the Highlands of Scotland, and around me rooks and carrion crows in particular seem the most ubiquitous of birds. They insinuate themselves into the landscape, gathering in the fields, perching on and flying above the trees, sitting on the lines between telephone poles and sometimes sweeping down onto the road to pick at roadkill – rabbits, pheasants, an occasional deer. They play chicken with the cars, taking off at the very last moment as cars speed towards them at sixty miles an hour.

Crows abound in Scotland. Rooks, carrion crows and jackdaws can be found in our woods and fields, magpies in our cities, ravens on our mountains and cliffs, jays in our woodlands, and choughs, black with red curved bills, on the islands of Islay and Colonsay. In the north of Scotland, the carrion crow makes way for the hooded crow, with its grey body and black head, wings and tail. In a space somewhere between south and north the ranges of carrion crows and hoodies overlap – and it's been shown that hoodies occasionally hybridise with the carrion crow. Here, for several summers I've seen a crow in the field, and there's just enough of a hint of grey on its upper back and nape to make me wonder. When I'm travelling north, I always look for my first hooded crow, though I know that the further west I am, the further south they are likely to be. By the time I get to Sutherland, it's the hoodie that prevails, although in the future this may change. It's thought that since the mid-nineteenth century, climate change has benefited carrion crows and their range has extended further north. Some speculate the biggest threat to the survival of the hoodie is this cousin, and looking at the numbers of these birds, we can see why.

The number of crows in Scotland is astonishing. Hoodies exist in the tens of thousands, but carrion crows and the smaller, grey-naped jackdaw number in the hundreds of thousands. According to the Scottish Ornithologists' Club's epic, two-volume *Birds of Scotland*, Scotland has some of the highest breeding densities for rooks in Europe, with up to half a million breeding birds that rises to a winter population of between one and one and three-quarter million birds, with the annual winter influx of European visitors. That's a wintering population of upwards of two million crows.[36]

glouk   the sound made by
crows over carrion

Once, up in Moray, near Culbin, I saw some rooks rise from a field and begin to gather with others – enough to catch my attention, but nothing exceptional. Still, something made me follow them, guessing at which unfamiliar side-roads to take, not knowing where I was going. They landed on the tops of a stand of trees beside a sports centre. It was towards dusk, and I watched, then filmed, their restless movements from stillness to flight, stillness to flight. As it grew dark, they took off, and when I turned to watch them go, I saw them join hundreds of other crows over distant fields, forming a kettling mass of black specks, their wingbeats unhurried, like looser, slo-mo versions of flocks of starlings or the flights of knot that swarm over the water just beyond the shoreline.

If I had not filmed them I would never think that I had seen that many. Now, even with the video of these rooks and jackdaws reeling lazily in the darkening sky, they exist as one of those moments that sit almost as a dream. Though I've been back to that place at the same time, in another year, I have seen nothing like it again, although for two winters, close to the Spey in the hinterlands of Abernethy Forest, I found the same phenomenon and watched thousands of rooks and jackdaws fly in waves for a noisy night-time roost on a pylon. They populated every horizontal girder and lined the adjoining wires for a hundred metres, causing them to sag. If something startled them and several took off, the reverberation quivered along the wire like a Mexican wave, causing a mass exodus into the gloaming sky before they alighted on the cables again.

Unlike carrion and hooded crows, who tend to stay in pairs or family groups, rooks and jackdaws are known for their gregariousness and tendency to flock, and that's what I saw and heard that gloaming. During the day, many of these birds can be found on the fringes of woodlands. What I saw that dusk in Moray was rooks and jackdaws gathering together before they poured into nearby woodlands to roost overnight in the trees, and what I heard was the lower guttural calls of the rooks mingling with the higher-pitched sounds of the jackdaws in outrageous cacophony.

Actually, words mostly fail to describe the insistent penetration of their calls, though bird books have to try. The Collins *Bird Guide* describes the call of the rook as 'hoarse, nasal, noisy croaks without the open rolling r-sound of carrion crows, more grinding and irascible "geaah", "geeeh", "gra gra grah"'. The Mitchell Beazley *Birdwatcher's Pocket Guide* states that the rook's 'prolonged "kaak" call is higher pitched than Crow' and describes the jackdaw as having 'ringing "keeack" and "kyaw" calls in its wide vocabulary'. The Collins guide further describes the jackdaw as having 'a jolting "kya", readily repeated in energetic series, harder "kyack!", drawn out "kyaar" and slightly harsher "tschreh"', though it goes on to note that 'details and volume vary with mood'. The mood, to me, seems always to hover between irascibility and tetchiness, and there's a perpetual restlessness to the air, in movement and in sound.

rook disturbance, uproar; a noisy company; a set of boisterous companions; a house swarming with inmates

The eighteen-volume *Edinburgh Encyclopaedia,* published in the 1830s, contains a more lyrical description of a chorus of rooks: 'The rook has but two or three notes, and makes no great figure in a solo; but when he performs in concert, which is his chief delight, these notes, though rough in themselves, being intermixed with those of the multitude, have, as it were, their ragged edges worn off, and become harmonious when softened in the distant air.'

Still, there's more to what makes these birds compelling. Perhaps it is their very blackness, and their other(ed)-yet-connectedness. Crows have always spoken to, and had a close relationship with, us humans. They speak to our humanity and our connections to nature. When I look at them, I see their intelligence, their co-operation and their power. How they control the air and wind currents above a stand of trees. But I'm also aware of their association with domains more disquieting and unnerving. It is, after all, an *unkindness of ravens, a murder of crows.* The language of crows pulls us into a myriad of different eras, frames of reference, attitudes and realms both everyday and preternatural, to the facts and fictions of them and how they continue to speak, and to crow, to us.

A *craw's nest* means a robber's den in old Scots. To sit *like a craw in the mist* is to sit in the dark. To have *a craw (in one's throat)* means to have a strong craving for drink, especially that induced by a night's debauch. In the *Edinburgh Encyclopaedia,* crows are described as follows: 'For the most part they are sagacious, active, and faithful to one another, living in pairs, and forming a sort of society, in which there appears something like a regular government and concert in the warding off threatened danger.' And though the word rookery now refers to their night-time roosts, in the eight-eenth and nineteenth centuries, a rookery was also a slang term for a slum. Thus Thomas Beames wrote in 1852: 'Doubtless there is some analogy between these pauper colonies and the nests of the birds from whom they take their name; the houses for the most part high and narrow, the largest possible number crowded together in a given space.' The anthropologist Claude Lévi-Strauss suggested that the raven was a mediator between life and death. Max Porter's recent and beautiful *Grief Is the Thing with Feathers* brings Crow to a father and two sons dealing with the sudden loss of a mother. Says his Crow, 'I find humans dull except in grief. There are very few in health, disaster, famine, atrocity, splendour or normality that interest me (interest ME!) but motherless children do. Motherless children are pure crow. For a sentimental bird it is ripe, rich and deli-cious to raid such a nest.' Liz Lochhead has a corbie commentator in her play, *Mary Queen of Scots Got Her Head Chopped Off.* 'National bird: the crow, the corbie, la corbeille, le corbeau, moi! How me? Eh? Eh? Eh? Voice like a choked laugh. Ragbag o' a burd in ma black duds, aw angles and elbows and broken oxter feathers, black beady een in ma executioner's hood. No braw, but ah think ah ha'e some sort of black glamour?'

Research has found that crows can remember faces and have

been shown to 'hold grudges'.[37] Other work has found that American crows have 'funerals' – or, at least, will stay close to their dead for a time, perhaps to see if they can learn what constituted the threat.[38]

hoddie, hoodie   a hooded crow; a hired mourner

Rooks apparently pair for life, and research on rooks seems to show that they remain in the sites where they breed – some rookeries are many decades old – and they often nest in the colony where they were born. Such reliability and loyalty to place may explain why in auld Scots the first Sunday in March is referred to as *craw-Sunday*, the date when crows traditionally start nest-building, or, as David Gilmour wrote in 1873, 'that day when crows commenced house-keeping for the year'.[39]

Old Scottish phrases speak of crow collectivity:
a craw's bridal
a craw's court
a waddin o' craws
a jet-tribe

A more ambiguous relationship, or perhaps distrust of them, can further be seen in the older Scots tongue. A *corbie-messenger* was a messenger who returns either not at all, or too late, and the adjective *hoodock* meant 'foul and greedy, like a hoody or carrion crow', or 'miserly'. Their presence, symbolism and, sometimes, their nuisance, has been noted over hundreds of years. P. Hume Brown, in *A Short History of Scotland*, writes that during the reign of James I (1406–1437) 'there must also have been great numbers of crows in Scotland in those days, as a very curious law shows us. Every landlord was commanded to kill the young crows every year, as, when they grew up they did so much damage to the crops. If the landlord did not obey this law, then the tree in which the crows had built their nests was to be taken from him by the king. If the landlord liked, however, he could fell the tree and pay a fine of five shillings'.[40] Crows are still considered a 'pest species' today, and, with a licence, they can be trapped or shot.

> *The cawing of carrion crows in the morning was thought by some to be an indicator of fine weather to come. Conversely, according to a different nineteenth-century source, if a crow flies over a dunghill, bad weather is coming.*

For all the gregariousness and sociability we see in rooks and jackdaws in particular, it's hard to shift the malevolence often associated with the bigger crows. Even now, the Collins *Bird Guide* describes rooks' nests as looking like 'large witches' brooms'. But it's the crows' relationship with carrion that defines most of our perceptions of their appetites and character. An old Scots word for a carrion crow is *gore-craw*, and the old folk song 'The Twa Corbies', or 'The Three Ravens',[41] describes the birds wondering where they will eat, before they espy, then feed on, the body of a newly dead knight lying in a field.

Back to the nineteenth century and the *Edinburgh Encyclopaedia* describes crow predation and their eating habits in florid detail: 'In spring, they greedily devour the eggs of quails and partridges, and are so dexterous as to pierce them and carry them on the point of their bill to their young. Even fish and fruits are not unsuitable to their palate. They often attack the eyes of dying animals, destroy weakly lambs, and, when pressed with hunger, will even pursue birds on the wing.' Rooks, they warn, 'not only attack the eyes of lambs and diseased sheep, but of horses that have got entangled in bogs'. Seton Gordon, writing in the early twentieth century, describes the voraciousness of a hooded crow: 'A newly-dropped lamb or a sickly ewe may be set upon by a number of Grey Crows, and the unlucky victim's eyes pulled out while the breath is still in its body. To the shepherds of the western coasts the bird is the embodiment of evil. To them he is *An t-eun Acarachd* – "the bird without compassion" – and they name him truly indeed.'[42]

And yet, although crows have long been accused of such heinous acts, the reality is that their diet is largely benign. Jackdaws eat mainly invertebrates and, occasionally, seeds and carrion, though they do also prey on the nests of hedgerow and garden birds. The hooded crow has been blamed for killing game birds and lambs, though more recent research has disputed this. Rooks, though they do eat carrion, also feed on invertebrates and, in the winter in particular, cereal grains. Some carrion crows, in winter, 'use intertidal areas to feed on shellfish'.[43] These are smart, opportunistic birds.

gore-crow   the carrion crow

More mystically perhaps, according to Jamieson's dictionary *a craw's court* is described as 'a court of judgment held by crows', and any time I see them gather in the fields, I wonder.

> Numbers [of crows] are seen to assemble on a particular hill or field, from many different points. On some occasions the meeting does not appear to be complete before the expiration of a day or two. As soon as all the deputies have arrived, a very general noise and croaking ensue, and shortly after, the whole fall upon one or two individuals, whom they persecute and beat until they kill them. When this has been accomplished, they quietly disperse.

In another version, Seton Gordon describes how a 'craas' court' of hoodies 'convened' every springtime in the Shetland Islands: 'A large flock of Hoodies appear from all directions. Apparently the court is held for the purpose of dealing out sentence to certain Crows who have been guilty of some offence, for after an hour or so of deliberation the whole assembly turn fiercely on certain individuals and peck them to death.'

The Reverend William Forsyth, in *In the Shadow of Cairngorm* (1900), recounts the story of a rookery in a stand of alders by a farm in Strathspey in 1826. The owner of the farm, a Captain Macdonald, wanted the rookery destroyed and hired 'a squad of men and boys'. The boys tore down the nests and the men fired their rifles to stop the rooks from settling back down.

At last the rooks seemed to recognise that they were beaten. They held a gathering in a neighbouring field. There was much cawing and conferring, but no reporter to give their speeches. The question was in due time settled. The rooks, as if acting under orders, arose and flew towards the alders, but instead of settling on the trees, they mounted up high above, so as to be safe from all the harm. Then they went through a kind of march, sailing calmly to and fro, and doubtless casting many a longing glance on their old homes. By and by they altered their tune. The march became a quickstep, merging into a wild, whirling, commingling dance. It was, as a spectator described it, for all the world like a 'Reel of Tulloch': -

'The dancers quick and quicker flew,
They reel'd , they set, they cross'd they cleekit.'

Then suddenly there was a stop – with a great caw-cawing. Then utter quietness. Out from the rest flew a leader, took his place in front, and like an arrow from a bow, started off. The others fell in line and followed. Suddenly the whole body winged their flight straight for the Boat of Cromdale, where, in the fir-wood over the Spey, they established their new home, and where, unmolested, they have dwelt from generation to generation ever since. The Highlanders hold that it is unlucky to disturb a rookery; and it was noted that Captain Macdonald, some years later, had reluctantly to flit from Coulnakyle, and to make his home at Clury, which he never loved so well.

One day, I drove again down the B-road past where I'd seen the mass of crows gather on the pylon and noticed that the electricity company had buried their cables underground and that the line of pylons was completely gone. There were a few nests on the small stands of trees and a good few crows still around, though not nearly as many. It's not that far away from the place that Forsyth mentions, where the rookery was removed almost 200 years ago. I wonder where all the crows I saw that evening roost now, whether they're all still together or have formed smaller murders.

I'M DRAWN TO EDGES AND margins and islands, and to what happens there. Inside and outside, within and without. Outwith. Crows are edgeland birds that flit between the fields they feed in and the trees where they roost, needing both spaces. I've seen twinflowers and common and intermediate wintergreens on the edges of paths, and even lesser twayblade hiding underneath an outcrop of heather just next to a track.

Perhaps it's the contrast, sometimes the surprise one gets when looking over from one thing to an other; or from the other back over to where you've been. The difference. Skuas skirt past the coastlines of northwest Scotland heading north or south, and the screaming summer seabird cliffs are their own worlds entirely. My urge towards margins and edges often coincides with an urge for the north: the Butt of Lewis, Hermaness on Unst in Shetland, Balranald on North Uist, Sandwood Bay in Sutherland. The island of Mingulay. Often, it's the pull of a CalMac ferry across The Minch. Twice it's been the ferry from Aberdeen to Lerwick on Shetland. It's that transit between places too, and what sits, flies, swims in the slow in-between. The storm petrels and shearwaters, the fulmars and gulls, terns and gannets. Schools of dolphins, a minke whale, or the split-second flash of a fin and that moment after, when you wonder what you've just seen – was it wishful thinking and just the shadow of a wave?

PART II

I N LATE FEBRUARY 2020, AS part of the Edinburgh International Book Festival Outriders Africa project, I went to South Africa. I chose to go to the southernmost tip of the continent as a response to my urge always to go north, and to see where some of the swallows go when they leave the UK. On my walk out to the Cape of Good Hope on the leap day of the year were the swallows that I so closely associate with summers in Scotland. They'd soon be embarking on their migrations north, though not all of them would be going to Europe or the UK. They flitted over the land and water, back-dropped by sky and sea. Though I was looking to the far south, to nothing else before Antarctica, the bright blues and the haze on the horizon fused sea and sky together in a way that reminded me of the views out from the northern coastlines I'm more familiar with: those Western Highland clifftops and beaches where the next land west is an island or another continent. And just like there, terns with their flashes of white sewed a line across sea and sky and moved low and purposefully in a way

I fancifully hoped would take some of them as far north as these places more familiar to me.

'We think of migration as a moving away from something unpleasant, when it is just as often a *moving toward* something beneficial,' writes Scott Weidensaul, and later: 'It is also the pursuit of the sun: the Arctic tern, which nests at high northern latitudes and winters in the extreme south, enjoys a greater percentage of daylight in its life (and thus more hours in which to hunt) than any other animal on earth.' He describes them as drawing 'a 22,000-mile figure of eight on the Atlantic Ocean'.[44]

In *The Frayed Atlantic Edge*, David Gange documents his journey kayaking from Shetland to Orkney and down the west coast to Cornwall, and reframes histories from this sea-bound, sea-centred point of view – how, in eras gone by, 'these seas were societies' arteries'.[45]

I once heard an archaeologist speak about prehistoric trading routes around the islands and coastlines of Scotland, and how what now seem like long distances and arduous overland routes between one place and another make complete sense when you look at them in terms of the sea and how people used to travel.

'To be in the margin is to be part of the whole but outside the main body,' wrote bell hooks.[46]

Edges and in-betweens become central and vital. There's nothing marginal about any place if you're from there.

uplicht

sapless	rainless, dry
lunkie	sultry: denoting the oppressive state of the atmosphere before rain or thunder
heavy-heartit	(used of the atmosphere) lowering, threatening rain
mare's tails	long streaky clouds portending rain
flobby	(used of clouds) large and heavy, indicating rain
goutte	a large drop of rain
saft	damp, drizzly weather
a stew	a rain so thin it resembles a vapour
a drow	a cold mist approaching rain
a smirr	a fine rain
a smush	a light drizzling rain
a dawk, a muggle	a drizzling rain
to ripple	to drizzle

a skeetlie	a drop, a small shower
a smurrack	a slight summer shower
callerin-o'-the-blade	a slight shower which cools and refreshes the grass
a drifling, a hagger	a small rain
laikin	(used of rain) intermittent
a dackling, a scrow, a dissle	light showers of rain
a borie	a clear opening in the sky in wet weather
a slud	the interval between squally showers
to skiffer, to spit, to dag	to rain slightly
to nyatter	to rain slightly with a high wind
to weet	to rain
weetness	rainy weather
a skarrach	a flying shower, a blast of wind and rain
scoutherie	abounding with flying showers
a blad	a squall, always including the idea of rain
a blirt	a sharp, cold shower, with wind
a plump	a heavy shower falling straight down
lumming	a term applied to the weather when there is thick rain

a blash, a plash, a slounge, a plype, a leesh, a rasch, a down-ding, an evendoun, a helm of weet, a tume of rain, a trash o' weet	heavy falls of rain
hale water	a phrase denoting a very heavy fall of rain, in which it comes down as if poured out of buckets
to lum, to dish, to team	to rain heavily
spleutterie	very rainy
to daggle	to fall in torrents
laughing rain	rain from the southwest, with a clear sky line
trashie	rainy, as in trashie weather
glashtroch	a term expressive of continued rain, and the concomitant dirtiness of the roads
a landlash	a great fall of rain accompanied by a heavy wind
glousterie	a day in which there is rain accompanied with a pretty strong wind
a steepin'	a drenching with rain
an uplicht	brightening after a shower
to appell	to cease to rain

M Y MUM HAS AN OLD anvil outside her back door. Heavily pitted, it is covered in a brown coating of rust, and has plant pots sitting on top of it. It belonged to my papa's father, or even his father before him. They stayed in Auchinstarry, a mile or so from where my mum still lives. They were the Forth and Clyde Canal's bridge-keeper and blacksmith.

Just up the hill from the canal stands a house called Castleview, where we think my papa's family, the Thomsons, moved after living in the bridge-keeper's house on the canal. It's a strange coincidence that the house here is also Castleview, the name of the terrace my gran's family moved to at the Haggs. Castleview – a traditional Victorian sandstone villa – is still there, showing its age now and surrounded by trees. A thick mass of ivy covers the gable end wall and encroaches over its windows, and I think the house must feel so much darker now than when my family lived there. My mum can remember its floorplan (*'there was a couple of steps down to the scullery and the back door from the kitchen'*) and the furniture and the times she visited it when she was a child, recalling in detail a fancy dresser in the living room and the dining-room furniture – a large oak rectangular table with two armed red leather chairs at either end – so fancy it felt like it must have come with the house, couldn't have belonged to us.

It's a house that has a resonance for us, even now. Even though the house was long gone from our family by the time I was born, my papa kept the walled garden next to it, and I remember the glasshouse there, and going down to pick the fruit that my gran would use to make raspberry and strawberry jams, gooseberry and redcurrant jellies. My mum remembers that our summer kitchen was always full of wasps, and when she says this, a flash of heat and the sweet smell of jam permeating the house comes to me, and I recall being scared of wasps from the time I was stung, just below my eye, when I was inside a tent made from a couple of clothes stretchers placed on the kitchen windowsill with an old rug thrown over them.

My papa inherited Castleview from his father and (so my mum thinks) was somehow persuaded by his sister to give the house to her. Aunt Liz Thomson subsequently went to a fortune teller who told her she would 'meet her fate alang east'. Looking for love, she sold the house and moved to Stenhousemuir. Where, it has to be said, she remained unmarried for the rest of her life.

nicht-hawk   a large white moth, which flies about hedges
in summer evenings; a person who ranges
about at night

ANY PLACE AT NIGHT IS another landscape entirely. Eyes strain and the tips of trees sometimes come into focus, sometimes not. A birch tree shapeshifts. Shadows rove. In Abernethy, at night, the forest comes alive with other species. Badgers and pine martens range, stags rut, tawny owls quarter and call, and moths – poplar hawkmoths, pine beauties, November moths – go mostly unnoticed and unseen, unless drawn to the light. For two nights one year we had a Rannoch sprawler – a red-listed giant of a moth, in moth terms – head-butt repeatedly against the windows of the living room.

In the summer, the light lingers into the late hours, and on a clear night, out of the trees, you can walk without a torch. In *the head of the dim*, the midsummer twilight between sunset and sunrise, the sky retains a lighter promise, a hope.

In these long gloamings, this twilight, woodcock rode over-head, and we've seen a pair of roe deer ring-dance in the field. Hares have come through the fence and sat in our garden eating the vetch and chomping down the yarrow like it was spaghetti.

Every summer I'm surprised again at the long hours of light that stretch beyond 10 p.m. Even after the sun sets there's more than a glimmer of light to the north, and a song thrush starts singing just after 3 a.m. It's always been this way, and I must have been able to see over to the Campsies at this time of year and night when I was young, but we were probably watching TV with the curtains closed, and either I just didn't pay atten-tion or I've forgotten if I did. I wonder if I notice it more now because of how we often sit and watch over the field for hares or deer, and when we look at the clock it's nearly eleven; or that I don't sleep as well as I used to, so notice the light coming in at the *scraigh o' day*.

In winter the place changes again. Night lasts for nearly eighteen hours around the winter solstice, and on some nights the moon sweeps round and through the bedroom Velux, shining like a spotlight; a slow panning and then it climbs way higher than the winter sun ever does, waking us up. On moonless nights stars seem like a Vija Celmins woodcut, and on insomniac nights I see Orion sitting outside the bedroom window, and sometimes I'm still awake to watch it set. When the alarm goes off it still feels like midnight.

ONE SUMMER'S DAY, I TOOK the train from Aviemore to Glasgow, then travelled north on the West Coast railway line, out of the city and suburbs, round the sides of hills, across moorland and past the geometric shapes of plantation spruces, pockets of clearfell, and occasional broadleaf woodlands to the sparse remnant Scots pines and on to the coast. After a summer in the forest I was going to join *The Song of the Whale*, a 74-foot-long sailing boat. I would be travelling around some islands with a group of people as part of Cape Farewell, a project bringing together artists, writers, musicians and scientists to think and talk about climate change and how we might respond to it. It's a trip that has stayed with me, in part because of the experience of slow journeying and hours gently unfolding. Days spent sitting, watching, thinking. We must have talked too, but I can't remember any specifics of conversation at all.

How odd to suddenly have that space around me, and a colour shift from greens to blues. The sounds shifted too, from the willow warblers and tree pipits of the forest to gulls and terns and the lapping of waves. Within minutes of the boat leaving the harbour at Mallaig, I felt an untethering from ordinary life and place.

The Song of the Whale sailed low and close to the water, and the mainland receded slowly. Any landmasses before us only gradually came into focus and with an altered point of view. Eigg became unrecognisable as Eigg from the north, and Skye from the south became a fortress. Due west, Mingulay would emerge over the far horizon, first as a watery presence, then gradually becoming solid. This was an unhurried traversal, hours and hours of simply watching and looking. Fleckit skies. No phones, no internet. Shearwaters skimmed the waves in black to white to black lines, posses of guillemots bobbed on the swell and skittered away or ducked under as we passed. Wheens of puffins. Solitary tysties.

On these islands, the past, present and future are intimately intertwined, and each island offers up all times, if you know what to look for. There are abandoned crofts and townships where roofs and walls have fallen, and sand and nature or the machair has encroached over doorways and into the crevasses between their stones. There are standing stones and prehistoric settlements, peat banks that have been worked for generations, the remains of old field systems that we see when a low sun casts its shadows, rusting cars and ploughs and tractors: all testament to the longevity of human occupation and influence. On Canna there's a Celtic cross from around the eighth century, which is broken, so I was told, because it was used for target practice during the Napoleonic Wars. Sailing around Canna towards Mingulay, someone pointed back and spoke of a cave on the west side where the island's boys hid when the press gangs visited.

There's a bittersweet tension between humans and nature that is sometimes balanced, sometimes lost.

Canna's shearwater population was decimated because of the rats that came to the island, stowaways on boats over a century ago. While the seabird colonies have seen a resurgence since the extermination of all 10,000 of them, the rabbit population, without predation, exploded and was perhaps upwards of 16,000 before thousands were culled in 2014. The rabbits not only affected present-day agriculture on the island; their burrowing threatened to destroy the archaeological remnants of humans who, though long gone, have still left traces hidden beneath the surface of the land.

These islands hold plants and birds that you would now be lucky to see and hear elsewhere in the UK. Red-necked phalaropes, corn buntings, storm petrels, eagles and divers of course, and it's on some of these islands that you might just hear the *crex crex* of the corncrake during the summer, calling from the midst of the tall grasses left for that purpose at the edges of fields. On some nights the gulls adjust their circadian rhythms to match the fishing boats that leave these islands before dawn.

Mingulay, more than all the other islands, felt the
most remote, unmediated, but also a place that had
been left. Left behind and left to its own devices,
despite the subtle marks that still remain and are so important
to acknowledge, and which place us in the grander, deeper,
longer scheme of things. With no ferry service to Mingulay
there's also no harbour to allow easy passage onto its land. *The
Song of the Whale* had to be at anchor in the bay and a dinghy
took us to the shore. Though there were old fence lines and
the remains of drystane dykes, paths were scant, and no one
told us where to go or what to see. The boat dropped anchor
off the eastern side of the island, in the sheltered curve of
the bay. We looked onto a sandy beach, a deserted village
and the land rising beyond to a smoothly curved skyline.

From the boat we could see the indents and humps of the
lazy beds and the priest's house, a double-storeyed empty shell,
sitting further up the hill and looking down on what had been
the island's main settlement. Here amongst these *lairachs* the
sand has piled in corners, and silverweed, thistles, ragwort and
nettles inhabit the ruins. Since 1912, when the island was finally
deserted, no one and nothing has stemmed the wear of the
weather or the creep of the sand.

Once on the island, three of us struck out from the bigger
group, maybe sensing a welcome break from the confinement
and togetherness of the boat. The possibilities of discovering
for ourselves was important, I think, though while we started
our walks separately, the natural geography of the island pushed
us closer together the higher we climbed, and we converged

just before the top. A good friendship started right there on that walk, and I'm sure that it was this place and our shared experience of it, the wonder of the day, and sharing that wonder, that cemented something before we even knew what it might become.

I should have guessed at the topology by the bonxies patrolling along the horizon line and how the sound of the sea swell rose, the sudden quickening of the air. But, as we neared the shear of the hill up from the bay, I expected to see over to a dip that would take us down to the other side of the island, maybe to another beach, but instead I was met with nothing but air, cliffs and water – and seabirds wheeling and crying below. My race, gender, class, age, the rest of the world, seemed to fall away from me, just a little, and in that moment I was exposed, stripped back, just human. Here below us was all birds: puffins and more puffins, guillemots and razorbills, fulmars wheeling high on the currents that push them up and over the cliffs so they sometimes startle, so fast and close and suddenly do they appear. This landscape, this seascape, these cliffscapes are vital, alive with movement and noise, and if you lean too far over the thrift-fringed edge of the cliff, perhaps to get a better view, or yet another photograph of a puffin, the reek of the guano rises to meet you. It is a place where you are both incredibly aware of yourself and where you are, while at the same time, small and lost in the environment.

After the sedentary, rich passivity of the boat, here was the gift of hours to just walk, to sit on the west coast clifftops, or dip down steep promontories to see the puffins and razorbills flying in and up, sometimes landing but often seeming to just tag the impossibly narrow ledges before falling away again. Perhaps they just didn't quite get the balance, the deceleration, the foothold they needed and had to fly off and around, come in again. We watched the whiteness of the kittiwakes gleam in bright sunlight against the dark cliffs in shadow, a shark basking in the waters below. Life pressed on life, and we entered into the lifeworlds of other species, overwhelmed by blue, black, white noise. It is estimated that there might be as many as 90,000 seabirds on Mingulay during the summer, and on the day I was there, there were perhaps thirty people on the whole island – our presence so fleeting. It was clear that everything would go on, whether or not we were there, indeed despite us being there, and as a gust whipped up to unsteady us and we found ourselves suddenly too close to the edge, or on a bank down to another cliff edge that was slippier or steeper than we'd imagined, we knew how vulnerable, how remote, how isolated we were.

Later, back in the bay, into and through the long gloaming we sat on the grassy banks above the beach, watching restless waves of puffins as they flew out across the water and circled and landed again and again until just beyond dusk.

In a forest, if you're paying attention and standing still, you can sometimes hear a breeze approach before it encircles and passes through and over you. In the same way, looking out over the Atlantic from a clifftop, say in Mingulay or off Stoer Point in Sutherland, you can see squalls form at sea, and watch as they come in and soak you, or reach landfall a little ways to the south or to the north. *Landlashed.* You're sometimes made aware, tangibly, of a near future soon to arrive. Might it be true that we see the future closer here on these islands than in other places?

When I think about the landscapes of these islands, it is as much about the space around and above them, the vastness of the sky, the sea-salt-wind coming off the Atlantic and the openness of the sea that can bely its power. Seton Gordon wrote: 'In its unhurried majestic speed, its tremendous strength, the Atlantic swell has its especial charm.'[47] As we sailed from Skye to Canna to Mingulay the sun was out. There were gannets dropping like harpoons into the water, the whirr of auks flying low or bobbing with the waves, Manx shearwaters speeding from trough to trough, gulls mobbing a distant fishing boat, and occasional terns too, and though we felt small and exposed, we were safe and secure and on top of things. And yet.

In January 2005, the whole of the West Coast was battered by a ferocious storm that did not abate for twelve hours. At its height the sea rose two metres and a family of five in North Uist, fearing for their wellbeing, tried to drive across a causeway to safety and were swept away. I remember speaking with someone on the island, six years on, who told me about this and said that any time a storm was forecast, people feared that it would be like that nightmare storm, and that fear was now something present in their lives. The island's inhabitants live with the human consequences of that storm and its aftermath, and perhaps they have already borne witness to what the future might contain.

In an article for Scottish Natural Heritage (now Nature-Scot), Stewart Angus and James Hansom wrote: 'Climate change scenarios for NW Scotland and the Western Isles envisage a combination of rising sea level, increased winter precipitation, and increased frequency and severity of winter storms.'[48] Storminess. Ben Buxton tells us how in 1868 a huge wave washed over Geirum Mór, a small islet off the south-western tip of Mingulay that rises 170 feet above sea level, and swept the sheep that were grazing on it away as it receded back to the sea.[49]

Extreme weather isn't new, but it is becoming more frequent, more ordinary, more regularly terrifying in places that hitherto have felt safe. We live in a complicated world that seems full of ifs and maybes, possibles and probables. The poet Susan Stewart writes: 'We live, like the rest of nature, in the present; and we live as well, unlike the rest of nature, beyond the discernible horizon.'[50]

And so, while some of us imagine, we can't *quite* imagine.

For others, the reality of climate change has been much more frighteningly present for quite some time.

There are places on the Uists and in other parts of the Hebrides and Western Isles where the water has come and pulled away at beaches to first expose lost and undocumented archaeologies, and then, in its relentlessness, has swept the remains right out to sea. These islands hold a hope for greener energies, through wind, sun, waves, even seaweed. We consider the effects of the associated infrastructure on birdlife, on sub-aqua life, and weigh up pros and cons, sometimes environmentally, sometimes aesthetically, and come down on one side or the other. These islands give and take, and we give and take: we come, and some stay, some go. Such places sometimes can feel too much and sometimes can hold too little.

Years have passed since that trip, and though I have been close to other edges, including up to Unst and to its most northern tip – about as far north in the UK as I could go – I've never quite had that same feeling again, though I came close, there.

I think of what it is to care. In places such as Mingulay, care was rooted in an awareness of how spectacular and special the place felt and should remain, as well as a personal vulnerability. I felt smaller and less in control, and had to take more care, especially knowing the ground fell away so sharply so close to where I stood. But what happens when such profound experiences are left behind and we return to an everyday that feels much more mediated and where we are too busy to pay attention in the way I did, and could, on Mingulay?

The next morning, we lifted anchor and sailed south around Berneray, and the wind caught and pulled us north up the west coast of Mingulay towards Vatersay and Barra, and it was the steady cliffs that we'd looked over the previous day, birdshit-grafittied, that dominated. Cutting along the base of the cliffs, we saw unexpected nooks and caves and arches not readily seen from the top, and I was struck by the contrast of the black cliffs in shadow and the flashes of the white of the gannets and kittiwakes as they drifted into sunlight and disappeared into shadow once more. Though I knew that the colonies of auks and kittiwakes were teeming up there, and I'd read somewhere that one cliff face could hold 5,000 birds, they were lost to us again.

fyoonach   (used of snow) a sprinkle, as much as just
whitens the ground

I'VE ALWAYS HAD RESERVATIONS ABOUT family trees – not because they're not useful or important, but because of all the things they don't say. Their importance seems to lie with how far back one can go, or rests on a particularly impressive or notorious ancestor, or we use them simply to find someone who is notable in some way. Family trees skirt over most of us, deny any agency or spaces for everyday lives lived – sometimes over long periods of time – and we become merely nodes that fingers flit over on the way backwards or forwards to others of more interest.

I only recall fragments of my family one generation above those who are still alive. That is to say, my grandparents' brothers and sisters, and then, only, really, my gran's side. My gran (born in 1908) was one of twelve. Her sister Liz, the eldest, was born in 1901 and her youngest sister, Mary, was born nearly a quarter of a century later, just over a decade before my mum. Some of this generation I know only by name: Gavin (b. 1922), who spent his time as a patient in Larbert Hospital, Jean (b. 1904) and George (b. 1906).

Aunt Liz Jarvie had rosy cheeks, criss-crossed with the thinnest of red veins, wispy grey hair pulled back in a tight bun and the kindest of eyes that twinkled blue. Her husband, Uncle Walter, was an ex-policeman, and I remember him being so much taller than my other uncles of that generation. They had a daughter who died when she was an infant, and there used to be a gravestone – a white marble heart – with 'Wee Jeannie' on it, somewhere in Kilsyth cemetery. That detail has always stuck with me. Aunt Liz stayed in a village about a mile and a half east of the Haggs called Dennyloanhead, west of another small town called Denny. When I was researching *A Scots Dictionary of Nature* I discovered that a loanhead was the upper end of a loan, and a loan was, variously, a lane, a narrow street, an opening between fields of corn for driving the cattle homewards or milking cows, a narrow enclosed way, a milking-park, a paddock, a small common. I visited Aunt Liz just before she died. She was in bed at home, and my mum recalls her smiling and saying, 'I'm helpless but not hopeless', but I don't remember that. I think there was a homemade crocheted blanket across the bed, but that might be a misremembering, and the only other detail I recall is her frailness and how she talked about the milk cart coming down the street; but I know I conflate that with a tiny photograph I have that looks like it was taken by a street photographer. It's of my gran and papa walking along a pavement, a milk cart with large wheels and a churn in the background.

Uncle Wull was small and bandy-legged and had a red nose flecked with coal dust turned blue under the skin from his days as a miner. He stayed down towards the foot of the town, and I seem to remember him always in a suit with a waistcoat, and a bunnet that appeared oversized, perhaps because he was so slight, and large ears that stuck out from underneath. He used to occasionally come up to the house, or I'd meet him when with my gran, when we were out to get the messages, but of his personality or humour, whether he was extrovert or quiet (I suspect the latter), happy or not, I've no idea. For all the quietness I associate with the family, my mum laughs telling me the story of how she'd drop her mum off at Wull's when she went to do the shopping, and how when she'd return they'd be screaming and shouting at the TV as they watched the wrestling that was shown on ITV on Saturday afternoons.

I never saw that much of Uncle Jake or Uncle Jimmy, and I can't remember or distinguish between them. One was thin, with a grey pencil moustache. Both were married to women named Margaret. One Margaret I remember as being kindly ('*Oh, she used to love you*,' my mum tells me) the other was known to be a 'nippy sweetie'. I can recall her thin, pursed lips and permed white hair, but not much else.

Aunt Martha (b. 1916) was about four foot six and feisty, funny. She had hair like my gran and rosy cheeks like Aunt Liz. She moved to Huddersfield with her husband Jack, who she met during the war, and when she came back to Bonnybridge, another village along from the Haggs, in her seventies, she brought with her a thick Yorkshire accent and a can-do attitude that she carried with her into her nineties. She died the spring after my Aunt Mary, who had waited for her to leave her bedside to die. In the family history that my mum's cousin wrote, he said, 'Aunt Martha during WWII went for a medical to gain employment; she had to have a minimum weight of 7 stones to pass her medical. To do this she put pennies and half crowns in the pleats of her skirt.'

Uncle Bobby (b. 1911) and Uncle Tom (b. 1913) stayed at the Haggs with my Aunt Mary (b. 1925), and these are the three of my gran's brothers and sisters I remember most and, along with Aunt Liz and Aunt Martha, most fondly. Those three Taylor siblings never married, and my Aunt Mary, only eleven years older than my mum, became the de facto housekeeper for the two brothers. Mum talks about how fastidious she was, how she had a duster in every room, and always had the plates hot for dinner. My mum says she remembers Uncle Tom inspecting the tines of his fork for cleanliness before eating. These little details. I wonder about the life Mary must have had. I think I can remember her laugh. I got the old sideboard that sat in the hall after she died; I wanted something of the house and my gran, the family, and no one else wanted it. It was so punctured with woodworm that, though we got it treated, they persisted and it had to be thrown away. I also inherited a low, upholstered Art Deco-esque chair with a drawer at the side that swivels out – apparently for cigarettes or a pipe and tobacco, not that anyone of that generation smoked. It used to sit in one of the bedrooms upstairs, and it's lovely, but if it was there or thereabouts in my childhood, it wasn't really part of it. It's not something I remember, but I cherish it for its connection to them.

When we visited the Haggs, we'd take the bus and walk down the short cul-de-sac and across the garden to the back door. A print of *The Hay Wain* hung on the wall in the living room and a mirror hung above the mantelpiece. My Aunt Mary would go to the press and pull out a box full of toys for me to play with – toy cars that were probably lead-painted are what I remember. Strange how my mum thinks back and can't remember there being any toys there when she visited as a child, and now I don't know whether to trust my own memory or not. Uncle Bobby was small, rotund and barrel-bellied, with bandied thin legs and, again, a small pencil moustache. All the men wore bunnets. Bobby was always more distant, grumpier somehow, and his temper seemed to simmer just below the surface. Uncle Tom was also small, but slighter, more like Wull in build, and had more of a lightness to him. He used to meet his cronies well into his seventies, and they'd go for walks from the Haggs to the next village and back. I remember he would play football with me out the back when he came to visit us in Kilsyth, his checked flannel shirt-sleeves rolled up, a knitted tank-top and his bunnet still on, brogues, I'm sure, on his feet. I can't imagine him inspecting a fork before he ate and getting grumpy if it was dirty. He loved cars and engines. I think all that generation of men did. My mum's cousin wrote that Bobby 'liked fast cars', as one of the points in the paragraph written about him – as if that gives us some clue to his personality or his being. One of the last times I saw Uncle Tom, we drove out to the Haggs in my new VW Polo, and

I lifted the bonnet to show him the engine, a fully contained modern one with nothing that he, or any of his generation, would be able to tinker with.

My Uncle Tom: the dux at school, spent the war in Italy, and would take his motorbike to the Isle of Man to watch the TT races. When he came back from the war, he drove a fork-lift truck at the foundry, which we think is what the nearby ironworks was then called. I wonder what opportunities were there for all of them, then. He used to keep his old Triumph motorbike in his shed (or was that Bobby?), and I'm not sure when he (or Bobby) stopped riding or what happened to it after he died. When Tom was in his eighties he still went out on his bike along the canal path and once fell in and had to be rescued. That same canal, my mum tells me, all of that generation learned to swim in, in amongst the dead cows and sheep that would occasionally fall in. And the same canal where, five miles to the west, my papa's father and grandfather were bridge-keepers and blacksmiths.

Sometimes, in that Presbyterian West of Scotland way of understated, undemonstrative love, Uncle Tom or Bobby would say goodbye by shaking my hand and there'd be a coin miraculously transferred to me. Still a teetotal family at that stage, or at least, that generation, when Uncle Bobby started to 'go' he would take off in his car and later be found in a random car park with a half-drunk bottle of whisky on the seat beside him. Eventually, when my Aunt Mary could no longer cope, he was moved into a nursing home.

Many of them were still alive as I reached adulthood, but as a teenager and when I left Kilsyth to go to university, my visits grew infrequent. Thinking of them now I have a sadness. My mum and I look at the birth certificates and the death certificates, and she remembers more of them, but I can't conjure much more than distance and space, a missing that could look like a hole if I were to peer too closely.

I think of these people from my past who are with me still, just beyond my peripheral vision – and if I turn my head I can just about catch a glimpse before they disappear. I have a longing for something that is a part of me, but I can no longer return to it, or them, or that time. However much I would like to see or talk to them, I don't really know what I would ask or what I would want to know. We'd probably just talk about the small things, because I don't really know what the big things are or how we'd get to them.

I wonder what it must have been like in those miners' cottages – twelve children in two rooms and kitchens – and why would you ever want to talk about it or remember how hard that life must have been? I wonder what kept them together without any major feuds or fallouts – as far as I can tell – though I am sure they probably had mini-resentments or life-long allegiances to some and not others. I wonder, as an only child, what it is to be one of twelve.

And I realise I'm still working with punctums, fragments of detail about things that happened, specific events we have knowledge of: Uncle Tom and Uncle Bobby during the war, the cars, the TT races, Aunt Martha and her weighted skirt. (I learnt the word *punctum* from reading Roland Barthes; when I look up its meaning again, I read that, in anatomy, the punctum is the opening of the tear duct.) But of my Aunt Mary and my gran, who stayed at home to look after and care for the others, what were the moments that defined their lives, that defined who they were? Because my mum went to work, my gran, who died in the summer between my first and second years at university, was in large part my primary carer when I was growing up. She'd have got me out to school, welcomed me home, cooked me dinner and tea, and I have, if not guilt, then a real regret I don't remember more of her, apart from her love.

Our family is quite quiet, reticent, I think, with no larger-than-life characters, no life-and-soul-of-the-party types – we were not the kind of family to have large, rambunctious gatherings. Perhaps we all have our moments, in the right situations, with others; but as a family it's not really our MO, and certainly wasn't for my grandparents' generation. I wonder if it was residual from being brought up Brethren, and what everyone was like away from their siblings.

No matter how many questions we ask that get answered, we only know their experiences, their lives, second-hand, once, twice, three times removed. The feelings, atmosphere, moods, jokes get lost, and I'm left with a vaguely remembered snapshot of sitting on a wall that says *England*, or maybe *Scotland*, from the time my Uncle Tom took us to Gretna Green (though when I raise that memory with my mum she tells me it was Uncle Bobby and he met us when we were on holiday at the caravan in North Berwick and took us across the border to Berwick-upon-Tweed, which makes far more sense). Or I think of another photograph I've seen, a long time ago now, that I don't have to hand. It's of my gran standing at the back door in a tweed skirt and a short-sleeved, knitted jumper. Maybe, still, after all these years, one arm's much thicker and more muscled than the other because of the scrubbing and washing and wringing she had to do of her siblings' work clothes, but perhaps you'd not be able to tell.

My mum tells stories sometimes, about the time in the Lake District when she did a hundred miles an hour on the back of a motorbike, or the time in the late 1950s or early 1960s when she and her friend Doris were sitting on a plane on a runway in Madrid when Franco commandeered it for his troops and all the passengers had to get off. They were put on a plane so old that they all got travel rugs for when they were up in the air. I can still see the woman she was before I came along, and she still has that curiosity and sense of adventure that belies her years. I think she's unlike anyone else in the family, though I suspect Aunt Martha might have been similar, and I'm maybe the outlier of my generation. Amongst the other family photographs, there's a yellowed cutting from the local paper, a photograph of a group of women performing in the local Women's Guild 'old-time music hall' concert, and my gran's right in the middle in a hat and a beaded shawl. I can't quite imagine her on stage performing, or picture what she was like in a group of her contemporaries, can't imagine who she'd have been when she was not a sister, not a wife, not a mother, not a gran.

a hearkenin' wind

wheerny	a very gentle breeze
pew	the least breath of wind or smoke; or the plaintive cry of birds
pirr	a gentle breath of wind
flam	a sudden puff of wind
puft	a puff of wind
summer-haar	a slight breeze from the east, which rises after the sun has passed the meridian
tiffle	a slight breeze or ripple of wind
caver	a gentle breeze moving the water slightly
kevel	a gentle breeze, causing a slight motion of the water
sawr	a gentle breeze
pir	a breeze, a flaw of wind
harr	a breeze from the east
darden	a dry, soft wind

piner	a strong breeze from the north or north-east
ouchin'	(used of the wind) sighing, blowing gently
whidder, blirt, gast, fudder, blouter, sob	a gust of wind
a glast o' wind	a sudden blast
flaw	a blast of wind
blaze	a sudden blast of dry wind
howder	a strong blast of wind
stoor	a stiff breeze
a reese o' win'	a high wind, a stiff breeze
to whudder	to make a whizzing or rushing sort of noise; the wind in a cold night is said to whudder
a whiddy wind	an unsteady wind, one that shifts about
bluffertin	blustering; gusty
cow-craik	a mist with an easterly wind, 'the cow-craik destroys all the fruit'
doister	a strong, steady breeze, a storm from the sea, a hurricane
swish	of the wind, to blow loudly and fiercely
beir	noise, cry, roar; force, impetuosity, often as denoting the violence of the wind
blenter	a boisterous intermitting wind
reaving wind	a high wind

gall wind	a gale
a glashloch day	a windy, blustery day
windle	to walk wearily in the wind
bliffart, flist	a squall
bowder	a great squall
houch	the moan of the wind; to hoot as an owl
sab	a gale of wind
blewder	a hurricane
a dreel o' wind	a swift violent motion, a hurricane
to grue	to sigh or moan like the wind
a hearkenin' win'	a comparative lull in a storm, followed by a destructive blast

The Constant Effort Sites (CES) scheme is the first national standardised ringing programme within the BTO Ringing Scheme and has been running since 1983. Ringers operate the same nets in the same locations over the same time period at regular intervals through the breeding season at over 140 sites throughout Britain and Ireland.

The Scheme provides valuable trend information on abundance of adults and juveniles, productivity and also adult survival rates for 24 species of common songbird.

British Trust for Ornithology[51]

EVERY SPRING, SO MANY BIRDS reappear after disappearing in the autumn, and it's only since the advent of bird ringing that we've been able to figure out their migration patterns. In earlier times, some creatures and birds would simply disappear, to reappear the following spring or autumn. Barnacle geese were so-called because they were thought to come from the goose barnacles that cling to rocks and emerge at low tide (and look at the heads of the geese and the colours and shapes of barnacles).

Martins, swallows, cuckoos, warblers, flycatchers and ospreys all return just as the geese are leaving, and bird ringing helps us to understand these constant movements and shifts and changes in populations. With even newer GPS technology, we know now that cuckoos take a different route north in the spring than they do heading back south to Central Africa in the autumn, and we know that some birds can return to the same area, sometimes, even, the same trees and nesting sites, after round trips of hundreds or thousands of miles. Ringing – placing a uniquely numbered lightweight ring around a bird's leg so that they can be individually identified – also shows us whether species are thriving or declining, and plays an important part in conservation strategies.

One early June, I followed a bird ringer around his patch – some scrub fringed with woodland that sits beside a wee loch, to the north of where I am now. We met at 3 a.m. and were at his site from 3.30 a.m., as he wanted to raise his nets before the dawn chorus. We were there until 1 p.m., walking in loops, checking each net, removing and ringing the birds caught in them each time. He had the most gentle and patient touch, for one whose hands seemed so big. Ringers have to go through a rigorous 'apprenticeship' that can easily take a year or more, practising under the close supervision of an experienced ringer before they get their ringing permit. I was in awe of the respect and attentive commitment he gave to each bird, how carefully he untangled them from the netting, how quickly he was able to ring them, and how quickly they flew away once ringed. Some of the birds were local, some had travelled thousands of miles: blackcaps from perhaps as far south as the northern tip of Africa, willow warblers too. How privileged I felt, and touched, to be close to these creatures that are so hardy yet so vulnerable. Still, as I look at the photographs I took, to this day I still can't quite shake an unease, can't quite reconcile the tension between the positive and important reasons for ringing – how the procedure apparently does not harm the birds, and the care clearly apparent in how the ringer attended to them – with the discomfort and the stress that *I* felt – that the birds themselves must surely feel, however momentarily, when I see how *caught* they were.

come-o'-will   a herb, shrub or tree that springs up spontaneously, not having been planted, comes of its own will; applied to any animal that comes, of its own accord, into one's possession; transferred to new settlers in a country or district, who can show no ancient standing there; sometimes applied to a bastard child

THERE'S AN OLD HORSE WHIP at the back of a wardrobe in my mum's house. Mum thinks that it belonged to her great-grandfather, who reputedly was a carter who transported supplies when the Forth Rail Bridge was being built. I find my gran's birth certificate: father William Taylor, coal miner, and mother Jeanie Taylor. I trace their marriage certificate: William was married to Jeanie in Blythswood, Glasgow, in 1901. William's father is also a William Taylor, occupation: carter. Though they married in Glasgow, William's usual address is in Castlecary, and Jeanie is from Banknock, the next villages south and west of the Haggs, and I wonder why they travelled so far to tie the knot. Mum and I look again and we see that they were married on 22nd February, and Aunt Liz, Jeanie's first daughter and the oldest of gran's sisters, was born three days later, back in Banknock.

I find an old OS map of the Haggs area online and zoom in on Castlecary. The viaduct that the Glasgow to Edinburgh express and all trains between Glasgow and Inverness still thunder over is already marked in this turn of the (twentieth) century map. Now, the M80 goes back and forth under two of its eight spans, and from underneath it's an impressive struc-ture. If I'm on the train south to Glasgow I'll look over and see the Haggs and Castleview Terrace, just before the cut of the motorway, look down to the canal, and just a little ways on get my first views of the Kilsyth hills.

The Castlecary station that is marked on the map is long gone, as is Castlecary Fireclay & Lime Works, and presumably the tramway that went from it to a wharf on the canal. It looks as though it's an industrial estate now. I look for Banknock Place, but I can't see any sign of it and wonder if it is now somewhere under the motorway.

The family rumour is that Willie Taylor the carter used to 'take a drink' at the pub on his way home, fall into the cart after, and the horse would know the way home. Mum found a photo and has written on the back, for future reference: 'This might be the carter reputed to go to Forth Bridge and stop at pub in Banknock. Whip for horse in back bedroom wardrobe.'

By the time it got to my gran's generation, at least when my gran was growing up, they were in the Brethren, an evangelical Christian church, though we don't know when this conversion to religion took place. My mum reckons it was during her grandparents' generation. She remembers hearing that in their younger years her grandparents were good dancers, and that must have stopped when they joined the Brethren, but we don't know what prompted this. In one of the boxes of photographs at my mum's house, we find an envelope with two tintypes that seem even older than the rest of these old photos and a photo of two men and a wee boy standing outside what looks like a miner's cottage wearing sashes and aprons. Although it's hard to read them, when I compare images online, I make out 'The Independent Order of the Rechabites', a fraternal organisation and Friendly Society that promoted abstinence (their motto: 'peace and plenty, the reward of temperance'). There are no names, no dates, and we don't know whether this is at the Haggs or elsewhere, or if the people in the photographs are our ancestors at all.

My mum tries to think about what her grandparents were like on both her mother and father's side. She doesn't recall much laughter or conversation. She and her cousin don't remember there being toys to play with when they went to visit the Haggs or any banter with the grown-ups. She recalls hating sitting next to Grandpa Taylor at the dinner table, as he'd tap the back of her hand with the teaspoon he'd just stirred his hot tea with. He gave her a row once for whistling on a Sunday (and her a female as well!). Mum sends me a note with some cuttings and other things she's remembered, including how her mum had to make sure her daughters were not in the kitchen alone with Grandpa Taylor when he was shaving with his cut-throat razor. Mum tells me this without further context.

Still, there was something there that made the Haggs feel like home, like love, and I suspect there was a closeness to how my gran and her siblings all got on, even if it was in that undemonstrative West of Scotland way, something I think my mum, by the time she had me, reacted against, and we've always hugged and shown love. I don't remember a particularly religious vibe by the time I visited the Haggs, and I can't remember going to church at the Haggs. Mum remembers riding pillion on the back of Uncle Bobby's motorbike and going to the speedway, and Tom and Bobby shooting tin cans off a wall with an air rifle. I wonder if it was parental deaths or the war that allowed a loosening up and more freedom, at least for the boys, that calmed again with age. I think about the sisters – Liz, Jean, my gran, Mary and Martha – and the choices in life they'd have had at that time, whether they were able to be who they wanted to be.

I wonder if one of my gran's acts of rebellion was to marry my papa, staunchly Church of Scotland, and if any of her family saw it as that.

O NE FEBRUARY, I SPENT A couple of days walking Abernethy with a friend who's an ecologist. She was recording crossbill calls as part of a survey to establish the relative numbers of each of the subspecies present in Scotland. There are three separate species of crossbills found in Abernethy: parrot, common and Scottish. The Scottish crossbill is now thought to be Britain's only endemic bird. Although the three species differ in average bill size, their actual physical differences are too nuanced to differentiate in the field. These 'Celtic' crossbills differ in bill size from others, and, more significantly, have also been found to have a distinct call (a distinct Scottish accent?), which was thought to be the method used by the birds to ensure that they only mate with other Scottish cross-bills – and why the method used to research their numbers involved recording their calls.

Such surveys demand a rigour that can feel at odds with the very nature of walking and being in these places. The whole survey area had been divided into subsections, each with destination points where the surveying would take place. Unlike a leisurely stroll, our destination points – where we stopped to record any evidence of crossbills – were what was important, and these had already been set out by the lead researcher and carefully marked on a map. At each of the points, a recording of their call was played to lure in any nearby crossbills, and any that appeared were counted, their sexes noted, and their calls recorded so that the species, common, Scottish or parrot, could be identified later, using sonograms.

The first morning, we walked on ice-encrusted snow to the first of the five predetermined points we had to visit that day. We started walking along a track, then veered east, through old pinewoods with the occasional birch, using a handheld GPS to reach our destination. Once we arrived, my friend set out a tartan, plastic-backed rug on the snow and placed her equipment on it: a tape recorder, a directional hemispheric microphone and a loudspeaker with a CD player attached.

We waited for ten minutes, scanning the trees and just above them, looking for movement and all the while listening. After ten minutes, whether there had been birds or not, she played a lure: pre-recorded crossbill calls played for two and a half minutes in each of the four directions, starting softly and slowly increasing in volume. If a bird or birds responded and arrived, we pointed the mic in their direction – the volume of the lure slowly decreasing while keeping the birds engaged enough to keep responding. At this first site, two birds flew in, and my friend pointed the directional mic to record the sounds, and where and when we saw them. She noted a male and a female, that they flew in from the east, and away to the south, and the calls we heard: FC for Flight Call, EC for Excitement Call.

We took the quickest, most direct routes to the next location point. With five sites to visit, our aim was simply to get there, and in the limited daylight our last stop had to be reached before 2.15 p.m. With our destinations predetermined, we had no reason to follow the more circuitous tracks or paths, and only followed them when they coincided with where we needed to go. Our walking sometimes felt counterintuitive, against the grain of the land. Mostly we went as the crow flies, as much as that is ever possible in this rugged place: once, we cut through an icy burn, and usually we walked off road, often stumbling through the thicker patches of snow that nestled in the hollows of the hidden heather underfoot.

It's a strange way of approaching the land, and we went to places that I've not been to since, and wouldn't quite know how to get back to. Fieldwork like this demands time to stop and listen, though bitter air and icy ground encourage constant movement. At each of the five points we had to stop and wait, listen, lure and record. This took between fifteen and twenty minutes each time, and the cold seeped in through thick soles and socks. Crossbills pair off early, my friend said, and even by this winter-bound February, she thought they had started. She thought pairs seemed less likely to interact with the lure than groups or singles, and I wondered whether such intuitive observations – repeated by a neighbour to me years later – would make it into the final research reports or remain part of the gut knowledge she carries with her as she moves through this place. We saw a few pairs of birds and a flock of about eleven, too far away and too flighty to record.

Though the landscape that day felt so still and bereft of wildlife, what the snow gave us was the traces of what had gone before, that, ordinarily, would have been invisible. We saw the imprints of roe and red deer, pine marten and perhaps, once, the footprints of a capercaillie. We caught the musky scent of a fox before we saw its track and spotted the imprints of a grouse – a clear line of tracks then nothing but two faint arcs in the snow, the last connection of feather to ground.

A couple of days later, on a day even more thrawn than the first, we went out again to do five more sites, this time cutting in from another direction, from the northeast. It was a laden day, the kind of day where the clouds above were dark and it always seemed brighter at the horizon. The kind of day that meant, despite wearing so many layers, I could not quite get warm. Waves of snow peeled across the land, though never so thick that you couldn't see the hillsides beyond.

On the track, the snow had an icy layer that held out for a millisecond before you crunched through. The first site was right in the middle of an area full of granny pines: old, twisted, gnarled, with a number of snags in various states of decay. In this older wood were lots of broken branches, the wood bright, reddish and raw where the weight of a recent heavy snowfall had snapped them off. The understory was thin, still grazed by deer and sheep, and there was little regeneration. Three crossbills were lured there – a pair and a single female, though they did not linger.

Next, we walked down through the trees and across a valley, the river meandering and sluggish. It was marshy beneath the snow and sometimes we sank into the knee-deep pits between the heather clumps. The Vibram soles of our walking boots sucked up the mud beneath the snow.

This was another landscape entirely. Eerie and still. A group of taller standing deadwood stood in front of us, and beyond them bog pines: small and stunted like supersized bonsai. Pale grey and spindly, they had branches at odd angles, like broken arms. The skeletal remains. The bare bones.

I thought about their shapes, and the propensity to remake them. We wondered at these snags on this river plain, the ones before, taller and in groups, grown to full height, and these smaller ones. Had the river changed course? Had the water table risen and drowned them?

The second spot was on this flat river strath, beyond the dead bogwood snags and stunted pines, with such a stillness and a quiet that even the snow seemed to pause.

The third site took us back through mature forest with more huge branches broken by the weight of snow, past an old stalker's lodge and along a track, back to the other side of the hill we had gone to on Thursday. Older woodlands again, but no crossbills at all.

That day in February, after visiting this last site, we returned a different way to the one we'd come and headed towards a pass that would take us back to the car. I was suddenly shocked by the fact that I'd been there before. After the last site, we'd been walking along the same track I'd been on that hot May day. We'd eaten our lunch at the same lochan where I'd seen the solitary widgeon and the single male crossbill in silhouette. This time, we'd approached the lochan from the north and not from the west as I had done before, and when we'd eaten our lunch, the view was completely turned around.

Though I'd thought I was in yet another new and undiscovered part of Abernethy, I was actually revisiting some of the same ground I'd walked before. It was not the expanse of landscape that rooted me again in that place but a simple fork in the track, with a small decline to a river I had not wanted to cross that day in early summer and the same one I had skirted past the previous wintertime in a truck. A memory of the sweep round I had taken, just before I had turned back, where the pollen had lain in thick yellow bands on puddles that seemed to evaporate even as I watched. I'd followed the track around, aware of a river and a path beyond it going to the east, wondering where it led but not going any further. I went back a few steps and took a photograph, sure then that I had taken a similar photograph from the same spot that late day in May, when I'd seen a pollen cloud over distant trees. When I compared the two photos, I was right.

With every step I flit between reverie and attentiveness, and the landscape comes and goes. Sometimes it's a birdcall that snaps me from myself, at other times, a trip or a stumble, or just something of the place itself. This is what struck me there and then. I realised that since my friend knew where she was going and how to get there, I hadn't had to look at the map to see where we were, so I did not really know where I was.

I was immersed in the day, our conversations and what we were doing, and hadn't taken account of where we'd gone, apart from an awareness of what was physically in front of me. There was also the shift from summer to winter, from warm yellows and greens to a bluey whiteness and a landscape drained of colour, to being by myself to being in company, from a meander to a purposeful task, and from heat and eyes watering with hayfever to eyes watering with the cold and a chill that had seeped into my bones. All these differences fell away, and at some point memory and experience overlapped and the place itself reminded me of how one walk can be put together with another and my own place-mapping occurred. The landscape itself put me firmly in my place.

After that walk, I didn't know what else might become of it. But the otherworldly bog pines stuck in my mind. Out of that day, through a slow, sometimes unconscious, percolation, I extracted the pines from their backgrounds and, eventually, several months later, three large etchings, the *Abernethy Suite*, emerged.

unco very; anything strange or prodigious; a strange person: a stranger; unknown; not acquainted, being in the state of a stranger; not domestic; so much changed as scarcely to be recognised; unusual, surprising; strange as applied to country; distant, reserved in one's manner.

Etching is a slow art, a deliberate, sometimes frustrating, sometimes marvellous craft. The nature of it suits me. Rebecca Solnit, thinking about walking, reflected: 'I suspect that the mind, like the feet, works at about three miles an hour. If this is so, then modern life is moving faster than the speed of thought, or thoughtfulness.'[52] For me, etching has that same feeling of being able to slow down and think properly.

On a practical level, etching is about how acid works into metal. Traditionally copper was used in etching, but as copper is expensive, I learned to etch using steel and nitric acid. The longer a plate is in the acid, the deeper, the thicker the resulting etch will be. It's like the way our understanding of places can deepen the longer we spend in them. Absence and removal becomes important too – the acid eating away the metal creates the conditions for presence.

There are steps that one must go through before getting anywhere near the final print. First, I'll cut the plate to size, then prepare it by bevelling the edges – filing each edge to an angle of about 45 degrees, first with a bastard file then a finer one. I'll finish with sandpaper to smooth the edges further. Bevelling removes sharp points and edges, protects the paper and the blankets on the press, and eases the press onto and over the plate and paper. Then, if I'm using a steel plate I'll use a sander to buff it to a shine. This reduces what's known as 'plate tone' – the default grey that one gets because of how the grainy roughness inherent to the steel holds some of the ink, whether meant or not. The shinier a plate is – the clearer you can see your face reflected in it – the smoother it has become and the less ink will stick in the areas you don't want any.

Once I've finished sanding, I'll protect the back of the plate from the action of the acid using a varnish called 'straw hat'. Then the plate is degreased using whiting, a fine powder which is sprinkled over the plate and turns to a paste with the addition of a little water. This is rubbed in with a spool: a wad created from the offcuts of etching blankets made of a thick, boiled wool and known as swanskin. These offcuts are coiled tightly together and sit comfortably, a finger-length long, the coiled roundness fitting perfectly into the cup of the hand. I love the feeling of the slight resistance of the whiting on the steel as it is held under cold running water and the whiting is slowly, slowly removed until the plate is clean and the stickiness changes to a smooth glide over. Once the plate is dried, the surface to be etched is then coated with an acid-resistant ground, and the plate is placed on a hotplate, onto which a waxy ground is melted then rolled into a thin coating. As the plate cools, the ground hardens. When one scratches into the ground with an etching needle, the lines drawn through the ground expose the metal that, when immersed in acid, is bitten down. The longer the plate is left in the acid, the deeper the etch, the more ink can go into and stick in the etched lines, the darker the line becomes (aquatint, a way of getting tone – think Goya, Paula Rego – is another story, which I won't tell here). These are, of course, just the basics of etching, and there are countless variations of grounds and other techniques to keep us printmakers continually playing. The photo-etching processes I used for the *Abernethy Suite* and my *walkDrawings* are variations on these broad principles, and use Photec and photopolymer processes, where light and light sensitivity take the place of acid.

The inks themselves, thick and unctuous, are scooped out of tins and flattened onto a cold steel work surface, then scraped with a metal spatula with just the right amount of give to create a thin layer which can be spread across the plate with a rubber squeegee. The preciseness of printmaking can extend to even the choice of black, if you are so inclined:

bone black
lamp black
brown black
carbon black
velvet black
vine black
soft black
blue black

And that's not an exhaustive list. Each will give a warmer or cooler tone that subtly alters how a print looks. Some are stickier and may work better on some plates than others. Bone Black, for example, seems to work really well on polymers, and generally is my favoured ink. And then there are the papers – like Somerset Satin, Somerset Velvet, Fabriano Artistico, Rives, Hahnemühle, Arches – which come in different weights and give whites of varying textures and tones, colder and warmer, that will shift the very atmosphere of the print.

The processes involved in etching, the repetitious difference involved in making each new plate, the return to the beginning, and the steps that must be taken in order to get to the point when the print can be pulled all require patience, but it's rewarded in spades.

And then to the printing itself. First, I'll select the paper, tear it down to the right size, if necessary, and soak it in a bath of water so that the fibres soften and it becomes more receptive to the ink when it's run though the press. I ink the plate using a rubber squeegee, coating the whole plate in a thin layer, then use a dabber, a leather-covered pad with a handle, to press the ink into the plate and the lines that have been etched by the acid. Then I use scrim, a loosely woven, coarse cotton fabric, to remove most of the ink. I bunch the scrim into a flat, smooth pad and, using a circular motion, quite heavy-handedly at first, feel the resistance of the ink and its stickiness, then use it more gently as I reach the end of the process. Once the excess ink has been removed, I'm left with the ink that sits on/in the image, that is to say, the ink that now remains in the etched lines.

I'm nearly there, but last, I take the heel of my hand and lightly wipe the plate, which somehow just takes off the last of the excess ink, then I clean round the bevelled edges to remove any stray flecks.

And as I write this, months on since I last made a print, I can feel the muscle memory. The give and stick of the dabber as I push the ink into the plate in repeated motion and its sound. How the muscles tense and twist in my hand and wrist and elbow as I wipe the plate. How my arm tires. How I am wholly within the moment of making. The final care of running a finger round the edge to check for a smoothness, the feel of the cold metal, the edge on the soft pad of my hand.

I'll have drawn out, on an acetate larger than the paper size, the measurements of paper that I'll be using and the position of the plate I need, so I know exactly where to place both paper and plate on the press bed. This registration sheet allows the image to be correctly placed on the paper. I place the plate on this acetate, blot the paper that's been soaking and place it on top, and then add a sheet of tissue paper. The blankets – one, two, three, going from thin to thick, to the swanskin – are placed over the paper. Then the print is run through the press – a heavy, cast-iron roller pushes through the blankets and presses them and the paper into the plate, and, again, as I write this, I feel the motion, the weight of the roller as I rotate the handle and it gains a momentum of its own that you can leave to spin. Then it slows and you grab the handle when it's still in motion and keep it moving and gradually slow it down as it reaches the end.

Once the blankets are lifted, the paper is peeled off, and it's only then that you can see what you've got. The print is placed between sheets of blotting paper and weighted down, or placed on the drying boards and taped down so it doesn't buckle, until dry. Then I'll tear it down to the size I want.

To make a second print requires you to return to the inking-up stage then back again to make another. This process helps you come to know the plate. We learn, through this repetition, how much we must wipe down, how much ink needs to be removed to get the print we want. The process of etching takes time, it cannot be hurried. It is a mixture of the messy (the inking-up) and the pristine (the paper, the final print) meeting in the middle of the process, on the press. It's only after the first print is pulled that I know if the process has worked. If it has not, it may be that the pressure was not correct on the press, or I overwiped the plate, or the paper was not right for the print, or too wet, or too dry, or it wasn't long enough in the acid in the first place, or the exposure was wrong for a photo-etching – any number of things. I may have to figure out where the problem lies, working my way back up the line to the point where I may choose to start again.

And there's something about that being in that moment of making, that though you are very much in the present you can also be taken to other places and times, and you might bring a fleeting and transient view or sensation to something that remains – those crossbills on that winter walk, the cold and the bog pines of the *Abernethy Suite* are with me to this day when I look at those prints.

M Y MUM'S GRANDMOTHER AND NINE of her children. Left to right, clockwise, are: Granny Taylor, Wull, my gran (who looks so like my wee cousin did as a child), George, Aunt Jean (my mum looked at this photo and said, '*Aunt Jean had that determined mouth all of her life.*'), Aunt Liz holding Jimmy, Bobby, Tom and Martha on Granny Taylor's knee. Missing are Jake, Gavin and Mary.

(b)othered   to be viewed or treated as intrinsically different
from and alien to; to have been made worried,
anxious, agitated

I T's ALMOST A CLICHÉ TO be a person of colour and Scottish
and to talk about being asked, Where are you from? No,
where are you *from*? – an intrusive and overfamiliarly presump-
tive question if you are not from an obviously white-on-white
nuclear family. Depending on my geographical location at the
time of the asking, my first answer could be Scotland or Glasgow
or Kilsyth. If pushed, and in the mood, I might say something
more. But as a rule, and as I've got older and more sure of
myself and my boundaries, I don't. At a book festival, in Glasgow
of all places, I gave a talk about Scots words and language and
dialect, Kilsyth and my family. During the Q&A that followed,
an audience member said (kindly, patronisingly, racistly), something like, 'You're clearly not from this culture – have you
heard of *our* Robert Burns?'. My mum was sitting in the second
row and we exchanged a long glance.

It's always interesting to read of others who deal with similar
questions of identity, or have their belonging called into question – even if we ourselves are perfectly at ease with who we

are. I don't think it's an uncommon experience for many of us (though that's not to say it's not tedious).

The US writer and academic Saidiya Hartman's incredible exploration of what she calls 'the afterlife of slavery' and her journey to Ghana to trace and explore the histories and narratives of slavery has at its heart questions about belonging as an African American woman. The book opens: 'As I disembarked from the bus in Elmina, I heard it. It was sharp and clear, as it rang in the air, and clattered in my ear making me recoil. *Obruni*. A stranger. A foreigner from across the sea.'[53]

She says later: 'I was born in another country, where I also felt like an alien . . . I had grown weary of being stateless. Secretly I wanted to belong somewhere.'

Jackie Kay writes of going to Nigeria and being called '*oyibo*', being told that it was a pidgin word for a white person: 'I spent some of my childhood wishing I was white like the other kids and feeling like I stuck out in Scotland like a sore thumb; and now, in Nigeria, I'm wishing I was black . . . It's the first time in my life that I've properly understood what it means to be mixed race.'[54] 'In the jumble of my features,' Hartman writes, 'no certain line of origin could be traced.'[55] The artist Glenn Ligon has made works based on sentences from a Zora Neale Hurston essay: 'I remember the very day that I became colored' and 'I feel most colored when I am thrown against a sharp white background'. In the etching and aquatint *Untitled (I Feel Most Colored When I Am Thrown Against a Sharp White Background)* the sentence is repeated and repeated, becoming almost illegible by the time we get to the bottom of the print, and I imagine how the bottom has been more deeply etched, using the acid to bite down and erase the text. Claudia Rankine writes of another version that Ligon made, this time repeatedly stencilling the sentence onto canvas with oilsticks and graphite. This contrast, sometimes friction, that Hurston describes, then Ligon picks up on visually in his work, is a strange thing. Reni Eddo-Lodge in *Why I'm No Longer Talking to White People About Race*, writes: 'I've been rigorously marked out as different by the world I know for as long as I can remember.'[56] Different. Still. I read an interview with Rankine and when she was asked if there was a denial about racism among black people, she replied, 'I don't think black people are in denial about racism. They just need to live their lives.'[57]

Closer to home, closer to now, sometimes it's in how the cursor has to hover over the tick box categories in equal opportunities monitoring forms: wondering what 'minority ethnic' actually means; how either/or categories don't quite work, or what they tell.

Growing up, I was only occasionally deliberately othered, or that, in any event, is what I remember of childhood and adolescence. Those moments of otherness never came from the place as such – it's always been familiar and known and neutral on the subject – but rather from the deliberateness of people around me. The casual racism and name calling of primary school never became more than name calling, apart from once, when a boy I'd hitherto thought of as a friend, who I used to play with when I was younger, threw stones at me – though he either had a very bad aim or did it to intimidate and not to physically hurt. I don't ever remember being physically harmed, though the racism felt more insidious in high school, with more overt prejudices that could affect my future life and self-perceptions coming from some of the staff and one or two of my peers. These moments still remain and come back to me at odd moments. The occasional, whispered 'darkie'. The horror of the hideous popularity test that was the boys choosing the girls for the Gay Gordons or the Canadian Barn Dance when 'gym' turned to Scottish country dancing in the weeks leading up to Christmas. Always second or third last, and just relieved not to be last. An English teacher not giving me any option but to be Nerissa when we had to read out *The Merchant of Venice* in class. The maths teacher who said that people like me didn't go to university. A PE teacher who berated my inability to do the long jump because 'you people are good at this'. A music teacher once said my lips were too thick to play the flute, and I think of the sixteenth-century Scots poem by William Dunbar, 'Of Ane Blak-Moir', where he writes about 'my ladye with the mekle lippis', which reveals not just that there have been Black people in Scotland through the ages, but how we could be subject to the same bullshit then as now.

Still, the average expectations at my school were, I think, more universal rather than targeted at me, though I had these specific instances to deal with. When I speak to my cousins we all have stories of the school at that time. And there were good teachers too – some art teachers, one of whom started the hillwalking club that probably changed my life – and an English teacher who introduced us to the poems of Norman

MacCaig, who probably did too. I remember those teachers and my time at school with a certain fondness, a certain reticence. Ultimately my desire was to get out and away from Kilsyth, and I left to go to university in Edinburgh when I was eighteen.

Mostly, I've been 'lucky' in that I haven't been beaten up or worse, though you never know when something might spill over, and part of you will always hold that possibility. Certainly, throughout my life I've experienced sometimes deliberate and what I've heard called inadvertent, unintentional, accidental racism/homophobia/sexism. Et cetera, et cetera. Sometimes you don't know what's coming, or from which direction. And that's not at all to say that those 'inadvertent', ignorant discriminations do not have effects that are, I'm sure, lasting. Even now, whether actively aware of it or not, if we are 'othered' in any way, we'll hold a tension in our backs, our heads, a muscle memory that's waiting for something to happen, or be said or done, that will cause us to step out of ourselves and become that other. I think about these noticeboards on building sites that say *It has been X number of days since the last safety incident* and wonder if we all hold these tallies within us. And here, on a day-to-day, week-to-week, even month-to-month personal basis (excluding what I see on social media or in world events), I can tally up quite a run of incident-free days. It's good to tally acts of kindness and generosity too.

Toni Morrison writes about 'the ignorant bully, the sly racist'.[58] Claudia Rankine and Beth Loffreda in their introduction to *The Racial Imaginary* write: 'One is always doing the math: Was it there? Was it not? What just happened? Did I hear what I thought I heard? Should I let it go? Am I making too much of it?'[59] Jackie Kay writes of childhood and, I think, beyond: 'I went home thinking up better retorts – which is one of the problems with racism; it is always, no matter how many incidents, unexpected, and so you never have the right answer ready. It often leaves you flailing and humiliated wishing you'd been quicker on your feet'.[60]

It can be the same with sexism, homophobia too. It's a thing that sits, is always with you, always an unwilling and unwanted acquaintance that can come knocking on your door at the most unexpected of times. It can be a loud calling, or one so subtle and yet so persistent that you won't always hear it, especially not at first. Or it might hover and not appear at all. In the heightened time of Brexit and lockdown, when I was living in the Highlands, something made me always carry a letter with my name and address on me, so that I could prove that I lived here, if it came to it, though I never, ever, had to – not even close.

Perhaps because there's just one of me, and, more often than not, I find myself in the minority, I've been seen as a novelty more than a threat, which can be galling in itself; and even within your hyper-visibility you can feel invisible. I remember discovering Adrian Piper, and reading about *My Calling (Card) #1*. Piper, who identified as Black at the time she made the work but who at first glance could appear to be white, handed the card out when she found herself in situations when she heard or experienced racist remarks. She describes them as being a 'reactive guerrilla performance for dinner and cocktail parties' and as being 'interventions to prevent co-optation'.

Dear Friend,
  I am black.
  I am sure you did not realize this when you made/laughed at/agreed with that racist remark. In the past, I have attempted to alert white people to my racial identity in advance. Unfortunately, this invariably causes them to react to me as pushy, manipulative, or socially inappropriate. Therefore, my policy is to assume that white people do not make these remarks, even when they believe there are no black people present, and to distribute this card when they do.
  I regret any discomfort my presence is causing you, just as I am sure you regret the discomfort your racism is causing me.

The critic Coco Fusco described Piper as dealing 'very precisely with her *body* as a "foreign element" within white dominated culture and public spaces,'[61] and I wonder about this, wonder about me. What do you do if you can't withdraw afterwards? What if I can't unremittingly deal with my body as a foreign element and don't see or feel my body as a foreign element when most of the time my childhood friends, family, cultural reference points are Lowland Scotland *white*? Except for when they are not.

In the time and place I grew up, very few people had encountered many other Black people, and any exposure came from 1970s TV shows like *Love Thy Neighbour* and *Mind Your Language*. It was a time when people would come to the door with books of 'black babies' that you could 'buy' for charity. Once, when I was perhaps nine or ten, someone from one of the town's evangelical churches came to the door to ask if I would present a book to one of their missionaries who was coming back from Africa. Why me? I wondered. Duh. My mum called me to the door and allowed me to make up my own mind. I said no, not quite knowing or understanding why it didn't feel right, but knowing it didn't, and though I like to credit myself with an understanding, even at that age, I also wonder if my rejection was partly to do with being shy and hating to be the centre of attention.

I write about the above from a panoptic view, and my childhood contained huge swathes of laughter and family and just being a kid. Times spent at my cousins' house, out playing down where the old railway line used to be, making a gang hut, a summer or two up at Loch Lomond the time my uncle bought a boat, trying to water ski in a too-small, borrowed wetsuit. Playing with all the other kids in the houses around me – kick-the-can and chap-door-run and Grand National, a game that involved running through and over all the neighbourhood gardens' hedges. Endless games of football, kerbie, three and in. Sunday walks. Playing tennis with my mum down at the Welfare (the Kilsyth Miner's Welfare and Social Club used to be in the building beside the tennis courts and swing park). School evenings spent going out for walks or on our bikes. Then, as we got older, getting the bus into Kirkintilloch and then, older still, going into Glasgow, to the second-hand record shop just off Great Western Road or Listen Records, a basement shop in the city centre. I don't remember any particular angst, or anything particularly prolonged, though perhaps, if I were to delve, or speak to my mum or my friends, they might say something different.

Jackie Kay writes of her upbringing and her politicised family, their awareness of the politics of race and liberation, her exposure to Black musicians and the civil rights movement. By comparison my upbringing was quite apolitical, though I think my mum has always been quietly subversive, in her own way, all her life. I like to think my gran had her subversive moments too.

I've been aware of Jackie Kay since *The Adoption Papers* was published, and have always been struck by those who've had a singular, successful direction or trajectory, perhaps calling. I feel now that I footered about for the first forty years of my life, couldn't quite find my voice or a method of expression. I found Kay again in the book *Daughters of Africa*, which came out in 1992. *Daughters of Africa* gave me two Scottish Black women of African 'extraction', Jackie Kay and Maud Sulter. Imagine! Kay is only a few years older than me, but in a world where it didn't feel like there were many Black Scottish lesbians, to have someone publicly writing and performing who was Black and Scottish and speaking about race, of course would have resonance for me. In fact, I don't quite know when she came out, whether she has always been out in her public life, or whether it was simply to have another mixed-race woman who had the same accent that first alerted me to her work. I remember reading *The Adoption Papers* and, of course, cross-referencing her life and background with mine.

Early on, I heard her read her poetry at what was then the

Third Eye Centre, now the Centre for Contemporary Arts, in Glasgow. Typically, I am still sometimes mistaken for her, though her hair is short and I have dreadlocks, in that way that people who see a mixed-race woman of a certain age with a particular accent don't quite realise there could be more than one of them in Glasgow or Edinburgh or at a book festival. Most recently, a guard on the train from Inverness thought I was her. 'Are you a writer?' she asked me as she checked my ticket, and I hummed and hawed because *A Scots Dictionary of Nature* was not long out and I wasn't sure if I could define myself as a writer yet. And then I realised that she'd mistaken me for Jackie Kay, who'd had a lovely conversation with the guard's parents on a journey they'd recently taken.

Jackie and I say hello when we encounter each other, though I'm sure she doesn't quite know who I am, and there's a residual thing anyway where, in places with only one or two other Black people, we notice each other and always nod or smile or say hello. *Who's that?* my white friends or partner ask sometimes still, and I'll shrug, often not knowing. Such moments of connection, of tacit understanding, are still really meaningful. Years ago, while I was at university or maybe just after, I heard Maya Angelou speak at the Queen's Hall in Edinburgh, and during the interval, I passed her as I was making my way back to my seat. She pulled me close and whispered, 'Stay strong.'

Even now, I will scan around me, anywhere I am, to see how many other people of colour are in the restaurant/bar/concert. And because of where I usually am, I can typically count them on one hand. I realise that I'm always aware, and pleased, when there are other people of colour around. One of the reasons I love going to a lot of places in the US, or the time I spent in Cape Town, is because I immediately felt like I fitted in more, because I looked like I might be from there, in a way that's not necessarily assumed in Scotland, and I can get away with it until I open my mouth. Even then, sometimes it doesn't compute that my accent is, could be Scottish, and I'm presumed to be from somewhere in the Caribbean.

In her memoir *Red Dust Road*, Kay writes about her search for her birth parents, how she travelled to England and Nigeria to seek them out. I'm not adopted, and though I read in Kay's book how it was not the done thing back then – to keep a child 'like me' – I was kept, and raised with a real sense of love and belonging. So many of us come from families that seem, from the outside, complicated or lacking, but from the inside are whole, and full of love. Unlike Kay, I've never wanted to delve into my African background beyond what I already know, and it's enough for me. I've always had a feeling that my family have been in the here and now, and my experience of difference has been rooted not in a 'minority ethnicism' (whatever that is) but in the varying discriminations that I may encounter. When I was younger, going up to the Highlands and booking double rooms in small, cheap B&Bs in folk's spare rooms, I was usually more wary of homophobia than racism. But I've always had an unshakeable sense of knowing that I'm *from here,* from Kilsyth, from Scotland, perhaps because early on I never knew any alternative, despite all the questions I fielded that assumed I was from somewhere else and occasionally being told to go 'back home', meaning, not Scotland.

As a family (and here I mean me, my mum, gran and papa), we didn't have a car, so mostly we walked everywhere – the dauners along the canal or around the dam. Sometimes on a Saturday me and my mum would take the bus to Glasgow or Falkirk or occasionally Stirling. I first went on a plane after I'd graduated from university. Childhood holidays for us consisted of a fortnight in my aunt and uncle's caravan – one year in St Andrews, the next North Berwick – and there I would go out and play with the fast friends I'd make for the duration of time I was there, holding my own running and playing football on the grass, revelling in being mistaken for a boy.

My Uncle Tom, and occasionally Uncle Bobby, would some-times come through to Kilsyth from the Haggs and take us for 'a run' – a car ride up to the Trossachs or Loch Lomond. I never really remember getting into the hills, walking in them (apart from up the glen) in that sustained way, until I joined the hillwalking club in secondary school. That club took me to places I'd never been – to Corbetts and Munros around the Trossachs and the Arrochar Alps. It opened up a space in my head too. What I remember most vividly about the hillwalking club were those days when it rained, so my cagoule hood was up, and not talking just walking, walking with the sound of raindrops reverberating about my ears, that feeling of being away from the town. Away from what? It might have been racism or maybe just teenage angst, or perhaps I just liked being *away* and in these mountains, like Weidensaul's reflection that sometimes migrations and movements are not *away from something unpleasant*, but just as often *a moving toward something beneficial*. I remember these walks also for the buzzards and ravens, the occasional eagle, and lugging my 10x50 Carl Zeiss Jena binoculars that I'd saved and saved for and mum helped out with, that I still have to this day.

Truthfully, though, I don't remember that much badness from growing up, not really. I remember these moments, pinpoints, pricks, punctums, *snags* – always more good than bad – but not much of the details at all. I look at old photos and I still have friends from school, though we don't see each other all that much now. Perhaps it's self-preservation that has made me forget the worst stuff, or maybe there's just not that much to forget. Sometimes, though, I wonder if sectarianism trumped racism, and the us and them was about Protestants and Catholics, though sectarianism never really affected me directly. Although, ridiculously, at primary school, there was a time when you couldn't wear green. Being good at football when I was younger got me away with a lot too. I wonder if it never dawned on me that I was gay and never thought to come out because I had enough to deal with. Perhaps, within the context of the visible otheredness I felt in Kilsyth, I simply waited to come out until I was at university and felt in a safer space, but that's retrospective speculation from a long way into the future.

ONE AUGUST, WALKING HIGH ON the Cairngorm Plateau, small groups of swifts came and went up and over us, slicing and screeching the air, moving north to south, arching, spiralling up and over, on their way again.

May-gobs   cold weather about the second week in May

IN ALL THE TIME I'VE lived in Strathspey, I've only seen a capercaillie a handful of times. Most recently, I saw a hen, pale brown compared to the black of the male, which flew off low and noisily through the brush behind me and to the side of the track I was walking along. It must have been close, and I heard it more than saw it. It was in spring, on the kind of early afternoon that is really late afternoon, with the early fall of night that occurs at that time of year.

The capercaillie is the biggest grouse in the world, and in the UK, it is found only in certain parts of Scotland. It is a peculiar bird and not often seen. They're one of the most endangered species in the UK. An RSPB press release of 2011 highlighted the rapid decline in numbers: 'As recently as 1970, there were thought to be as many as 20,000 individual birds but by the early 1990s, when the first formal surveys were conducted, numbers had declined sharply, in particular in Deeside and Perthshire . . . [a] census conducted in 2004, found that there were an estimated 1,980 birds remaining in Scotland. This compared to an estimate of just 1,073 birds in 1988–1989 which triggered targeted conservation action for the species.'[62] A press release from Cairngorms National Park Authority in June 2021 discusses new data from lek counts which showed another 35% decline between 2015 and 2021.[63]

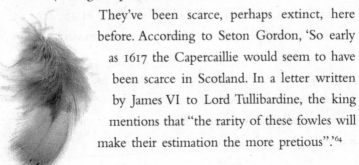

Here in Strathspey, its stronghold, the capercaillie is a storied bird, and I've seen it described as 'charismatic' and one of Scotland's 'iconic' species. It is often likened to a turkey: big, awkward and in its own way quite compelling. Known for their mating displays, in years gone by, these springtime leks got the keenest birdwatchers up before dawn for a visit to Loch Garten Nature Centre, which would open throughout April and May at 5 a.m. for a lek that was just in front of the hide. I went once or twice and it was crammed with birders jostling for position.

They've been scarce, perhaps extinct, here before. According to Seton Gordon, 'So early as 1617 the Capercaillie would seem to have been scarce in Scotland. In a letter written by James VI to Lord Tullibardine, the king mentions that "the rarity of these fowles will make their estimation the more pretious".'[64]

By the 1750s they were known to be rare in Scotland, and by the early 1800s thought to be extinct. However, the birds were reintroduced in the 1830s, when the Marquis of Breadalbane imported twenty-four birds from Sweden and set them free.

This reintroduction was incredibly successful, and the birds continued to thrive until well into the twentieth century. In the late 1960s, the naturalists Desmond Nethersole-Thompson and Adam Watson were able to write: 'Foresters dislike caper-caillie because they damage young trees by removing shoots and buds. Some foresters even drive along the forest roads to shoot them with .22 rifles at point-blank range out of their car windows.'[65] I once spoke with a man who had been a warden at the Loch Garten Nature Centre in the late 1960s, and he said he remembered seeing capers in the woods and along the sides of the road. It never crossed his mind, back then, he said, to have to worry about them.

How quickly things can change, become precarious. It seems there is no straightforward answer to their more recent decline. Among the suggested causes are: predation, in particular by the pine marten, which is itself a protected species; the structure of the forest and its understory – heather-heavy versus a predominance of blaeberry; the collision risk of the fencing that was erected to stop deer browsing new growth and thus allow regeneration; changes in climate and the impact of wetter springs on new broods; how (their now) low numbers (and the potentially low gene pool) together with the fragmented nature of our forests might impact on their viability; human interference and disturbance, including the increased use of mountain bikes and walking, often with dogs, through their habitats. Most likely, it is a mixture of all these things, and there are many initiatives at play to try to mitigate their decline.

For years, one of the rites of summer in Abernethy was brood counting – mapping the reserve and walking parcels of it each year in order to estimate their numbers. It's an activity that again helped me to see and understand Abernethy in a different way. It took me to places that I've never been back to again, and would probably not be able to find by myself. There's a quiet rigour to brood counting that, like when I followed my ecologist friend as she surveyed crossbills, was dependent on, but independent of, the landscape at the same time, in terms of how the area had been mapped out to ensure coverage. Every day, we'd cover two or three different areas. We would go to specified starting points, then stand in a line, with an evenly spaced distance between us. Usually, we would start along a roadside or a path, and then walk in, through the trees. This first day, there were six people – a mixture of rangers and volunteers – and two dogs. The rangers checked their two-way radios, then with one last look at the map, we'd set off, walking in straight lines as far as possible, irrespective of contours: some of us climbed slopes while others walked through hollows; some of us walked through heather while others bracken patches. Always, we tried to keep equally spaced. Sometimes a bog or a thicket of juniper got in the way and we had to come together around its edges before fanning out again on the other side. Periodically, there would be a faint cry of 'bird away' and we'd stop to look in the direction of the call for any movement through the trees, trying to identify what had been flushed up, and if it *was* a capercaillie, whether cock, hen or chick.

I first went brood counting in 2011, and that year, the weather prior to the first day had been cold and wet, and thundery downpours had punctuated the last ten days before. One of the rangers said that he could not remember a wetter, cooler summer. Expectations for the numbers of birds we would see were not high.

From the drier, forested ground where we started, we came to stunted, half-drowned bog pines with their saturated roots and dwarfed growth steeped in mirky water. At the end of that first sweep, we came across no capercaillies or any signs of them, though someone noticed a buzzard's nest with two chicks in it, and a couple of jays, perhaps just passing through.

On the second site, an area just north of the first, we started the sweep eastwards, or maybe more northeast. Plantation pines again, old, though, and we walked through, past occasional granny pines with their thickset trunks and wilder branches interrupting the uniform, vertical rigour of the plantation trees. Those of us at the more southern end stopped and waited while those who started to the north swept round, carrying on east, then turning south and back westwards again, back around us so we made a circle, or a loop, of sorts. I can imagine the view from above, like some kind of raggedy

Ziegfeld Follies, working around a fulcrum back to where we started. Again, no capers, but we heard a buzzard or two, some finches and a flurry of tits including a crestie, and as we got back to the trucks we heard the peep of a common sandpiper in the woods just across the road from the loch.

On these first two days, we came across nothing except for a couple of cock feathers – primaries, black, square-ended with flecks of white. I noticed that the blaeberries were out, and saw creeping ladies' tresses, a pinewood species of orchid – subtle, understated, but, in these pinewoods, not too rare.

On the third day, we scoured a planted pinewood area. The woods we walked through that day were, for the most part, blaeberry-heavy, then the balance would shift more to heather, then back to blaeberry and very occasionally, where wetter, to mosses and sphagnums, and back to heather and occasional tangles of juniper. Through the heather, the scarlet of cowberries, the yellows of cow-wheat and tormentil and tiny white clutches of northern bedstraw would appear.

Much of this kind of work is to do with looking for signs. I've also walked with an ecologist looking for scat to try to estimate the numbers of pine martens, and with a forester looking to see where the tips of young trees had been browsed by deer. Here, if we came across no birds, it was most likely feathers that would signify their presence or activity. In one particular area with a lot of blaeberries, we came across a lot of small white feathers, but these belonged to woodpigeons who, like any capers, would be feasting on the fruit.

On the days there were dogs, they'd run ahead of the line,

sometimes following a scent back around behind us and then nosing in front again. When the scent was strong and fresh, they would stop dead, nose pointing, and wait for their owner to approach and coax them to follow the scent, find the bird. Capercaillie, particularly mothers with chicks, will lie low until the last minute before striking off. If she has no chicks, the hen will fly quite a ways away, but if she is with chicks, she is most likely to fly up, then to a nearby tree, to stay nearer her brood. One of the dogs flushed up a chick from under a juniper bush and kept sniffing around, all the while encouraged by his owner to 'go on . . . go on . . .' until the mother was flushed up as well. The ranger asked, 'All gone? All gone?' as the dog sniffed, looking for more traces, more birds, but there were no more to be found.

Sometimes, when we waited as the dogs searched, it was so still that the only sounds came from the occasional rustle of the dogs amidst the heather and bracken if they came near, and birds in the trees – tits mainly, and occasionally on lower ground a wren, chaffinches and, once or twice, crossbills that flew overhead. On such days, midges piled in around our heads the minute we stopped. One day, a herd of about ten red deer bounded away, below us.

During one sweep, higher up in the smirr, some of us walked to the top of the hill while others swept around its slope, and we found a couple of feathers. A hen caper was startled up by those further down, but we were too high up to see her. We heard a buzzard's hollow mewing overhead, and the call of a woodpecker, and saw the rain grey the hills to the south and approach us again. We walked back down through plantation pines, straight and regulated, and we saw where, a year or so before, the occasional tree had been pulled down and left to create the dead and dying wood that would create microhabitats for other species, and, with its roots exposed, provide shelter for any caper or other creatures that wanted it.

We walked very much by ourselves but with an awareness of the people on either side, each adjusting our paths and trying to keep an equidistance between us. Sometimes, it felt that there were no birds, and no hope, but other sweeps pulled up two or three birds, and an optimism that we would find more.

Sometimes, after walking and coming across very little, when I'd got into the rhythm of walking and everything felt settled and calm, a capercaillie would be flushed up. The sudden movement and noise would cause my heart to leap as its wingbeats clap-rustled the air like a panic.

On another day, we went to a different area and walked through old pinewoods with an understory of heather and blaeberry again, and it gradually shifted from heather underfoot to a long, dewy grass: thick and the brightest of greens. It was a place where there had been a settlement until the 1870s, and this had been the sward where the sheep had grazed. In that small space of time after the sheep had been removed and before deer numbers grew, a number of trees were able to seed and 'get away' before the deer became a problem for them. When the deer came, fewer trees could get away, but those that did, remain.

These trees now stand in essentially what used to be a meadow, and there are moss-covered walls and remnants of old buildings there, right in the middle of these woods, and hidden by them. In a line, we swept through and past, we didn't stop, and in all the walks I've taken since, I've never come across that place again. I imagine that it's tucked in somewhere near where I stay, and it's funny how walking in these lines and in these loops make some parts of the forest fit together, while other parts feel completely alien, a new place completely.

On our last sweep, one bird flew up right in front of me, but it was so quick and low through the bracken and branches I couldn't see it, though I heard its wings and almost felt the air shift as it moved. Another (perhaps two) flew up and away ahead of somebody next to me, soft grey feathers revealing where the birds had been. We continued walking in our line, back down to the trucks, finding no more.

I spoke with a ranger who was rethinking brood counting. He reckoned that they already knew capercaillie numbers were low and what needed to be done so that their numbers might increase. He wondered whether, given the low numbers, any disturbance, including brood counting, was necessary every year or whether there might be other, better ways. I hope that whenever, and however, they do the next count, there will be a pleasant surprise, though I suspect we'll need a long time to turn the numbers around. I think again of the project with a 200-year vision to expand and connect these forests, and hope it's not too late for these birds.

Still, every spring, as swallows and house martins return and the sounds of place change with the songs of willow warblers and tree pipits and the calls of cuckoos, I watch the weather and wonder, when there's May-gobs or an extended run of rain, if these birds, so rarely seen and so rare, are making their way in the heart of the forest, and how their chicks are faring. I wonder as I walk these woods when the next time I see one will be.

IN SPRING, JUST BEFORE DUSK, brown hares arrive in the field, and as spring moves to summer, leverets will join them. Sometimes they're alert to the briefest movement in the shadows of the house and dart away, but if we're still or move slowly, they'll sit in the field for hours.

We've watched the hares feed and teach the leverets how to zig and zag to avoid predators, and we've seen them grow to a size which they can no longer squeeze through the stock fencing to get into the garden. They appear just as dusk is falling, and in the fading light, they look like the stubs of rushes that lie in clumps amidst rough tussocks of grass.

They're here after dark too – I catch them, sometimes, on a motion sensor nature camera that I set up in the corner of the garden facing onto the field. They move so fast that they're in and out of the frame before it's triggered, the back of their hind leg the only thing caught.

At the very cusp of night, when the bracken at the edge of the trees is on the turn, sometimes you can't tell the difference between it and the roe deer that browse amongst it. In autumn, I've almost stood on a snipe as it hunkered down in exactly the same tones as bracken and shade before it flew off with a heart-stopping rustle and shake.

neither one thing or the other[66]

ambivalence	the coexistence in one person of contradictory emotions or attitudes (as love and hatred) towards a person or thing
between the sun and the sky	the interval between daybreak and sunrise
brackish	of a somewhat salt or saline taste; partly fresh, partly salt; *figurative and transformed*; spoilt by mixture, as of seawater with freshwater; nauseous, distasteful
coconut	*slang (depreciative)*, a non-white or dark-skinned person who is perceived as adopting or identifying with white culture as opposed to his or her own ethnic culture
coexistence	existence together or in conjunction; with special reference to peaceful existence side by side of states professing different ideologies
ecotone	a transitional area between two or more distinct ecological communities

forenicht the early part of the night; the interval between twilight and bedtime

foreshore the fore part of the shore; that part which lies between the high- and low-water marks; occasionally the ground lying between the edge of the water and the land which is cultivated or built upon

grey area an intermediate area between two opposing positions; a situation, subject, etc., not clearly or easily defined, or not covered by an existing category or set of rules; (*U.S.*) a residential area which is somewhat affected by poverty but not regarded as a slum; (*South Africa*) a residential area inhabited without segregation by people of differing ethnic backgrounds, despite apartheid laws. Now *hist.*

half caste a mixed caste; a race sprung from the union of two castes or races; a person of mixed descent

head of the dim midsummer twilight between sunset and sunrise

hybrid the offspring of two animals or plants of different species or (less strictly) varieties; a half-breed, cross-breed, or mongrel

hyphen a short dash or line (-) used to connect two words together as a compound; also, to join the separated syllables of a word, as at the end of a line; or to divide a word into parts for etymological or other purpose; a small connecting link

intersectionality   the interconnected nature of social categorisations such as race, class and gender, regarded as creating overlapping and interdependent systems of discrimination or disadvantage; a theoretical approach based on such a premise

interstice   an intervening space (usually, empty); *esp.* a relatively small or narrow space, between things or the parts of a body (frequently in *plural*, the minute spaces between the ultimate parts of matter); a narrow opening, chink, or crevice; an intervening space of time; an interval between actions. Now *rare*

liminal   characterised by being on a boundary or threshold, esp. by being transitional or intermediate between two states, situations, etc.; (*cultural anthropology*) of or relating to a transitional or intermediate state between culturally defined stages of a person's life, esp. as marked by a ritual or rite of passage; characterised by liminality

margin   an edge, a border; that part of a surface which lies immediately within its boundary, esp. when in some way marked off or distinguished from the rest of the surface; the ground immediately adjacent to a river or body of water; a river bank, a shore, etc.; the space on a page, etc., between its extreme edge and the main body of writing or printed matter (sometimes containing notes, references, illuminations etc.); a region or point of transition between states, epochs, etc.; a moment in time when some change or occurrence is imminent; a limit below or beyond which something ceases to be feasible

mezzotint an engraving technique developed in the seventeenth century which allows for the creation of prints with soft gradations of tone and rich and velvety blacks. The process involves indenting the metal printing plate by rocking a toothed metal tool across the surface. Each pit holds ink and if printed at this stage the image would be solid black. However, the print-maker creates dark and light tones by gradually rubbing down or burnishing the rough surface to various degrees of smoothness to reduce the ink-holding capacity of areas of the plate

mixed with nouns, forming compounds used *attributively* with the sense 'having or involving a mixed ———', or 'having a mixture of types of ———'; mixed-ability; mixed-race

mulatto a person having one white and one black parent; frequently more generally: a person of mixed race resembling a mulatto; of the colour of the skin of a mulatto; tawny; *mulatta* a woman with one black and one white parent. Now *chiefly considered offensive*

neb-o'-the-morning	the time between dawn and sunrise
oreo	*U.S. slang* (*depreciative*) in African-American usage: an African-American who adopts or identifies with middle-class white culture as opposed to urban African-American culture
strandline	the land bordering a sea, lake, or river; in a more restricted sense, that part of a shore which lies between the tide-marks; sometimes used vaguely for coast, shore
sockin-hour	the portion of time between day-light and candle light
stray	lost; not at home; strange
twilight	the light diffused by the reflection of the sun's rays from the atmosphere before sunrise, and after sunset; the period during which this prevails between daylight and darkness; most commonly applied to the evening twilight, from sunset to dark night; morning twilight, which lasts from daybreak to sunrise

> *bobber*   in fly-fishing, the hook which plays loosely on
> the surface of the water, as distinguished from the
> *trailer*, at the extremity of the line

I HAVE A BOOK OF MY papa's fishing flies that I've had since he died, and it has sat in an old box of stuff for years. It's so full that it doesn't close at all; instead it bulges open at 45 degrees with a cover made of the thinnest leather that has become separated and flails now as an ineffective skin. Sometimes he would get up early in the morning, gather his rod and his green fishing jacket, throw on his tweed bunnet which he never left the house without, get his rubber waders and a wicker fishing basket, and that would be him for the day. He would bring back trout, which he'd gut in the kitchen sink. He used to walk down over the Couches to the Stirling Road and catch the bus to Stirling, then another that would take him somewhere towards Rumbling Bridge, which seems like a hell of a way to go. My mum once said that my gran hated him going fishing because she'd had a miscarriage when he'd been away. Another story told in passing that holds so much but gives nothing more.

I'd always thought the fly book was my papa's, but my neighbour up here comes to look at the flies and tells me that these are very traditional flies that look to date from around the 1920s and '30s. He thinks my papa probably inherited them, though I'm not so sure, or perhaps made them in his youth. My neighbour thinks they are for trout and maybe the odd grayling (a small, river-bound fish). The flies are all small sizes – 14, 16, maybe as small as 18 – and yes, I think: modest flies for modest expectations. They've all seen better days because they've been crushed together in pockets and bags and drawers and boxes and hadn't seen the light of day in years until I dug them out. And they are, after all, at least fifty or sixty years old, maybe older, and there's a sprinkling of black dust on some of the pages where there have been mites in amongst them.

My neighbour tells me that they are mostly dry flies – those that you use to fish on the surface – but there are some wet flies that will sink under the surface of the water to tease the fish below. A few flies and casts are already made up, ready for use. They're all hooked into ancient felt pages that have also seen better days, or wrapped around pieces of card that have been carefully cut and notched, to hold both the flies and the line. It looks like they are from old Scott's Porage Oats boxes and shortbread packets, and I suddenly have a flash of my gran making porridge in the mornings, thin swirls of ice on the insides of the windows in the coldest of winter days, and my papa telling me about Jack Frost.

They used to make flies from the feathers of certain birds, my neighbour says, like mallard and teal, partridge and pheasant, and from hare's lugs, and I wonder where my papa gathered the feathers he needed.

'He's probably been fishing in small rivers – there's a wee lure here. That's got a wee propeller on it and it spins in the water,' my neighbour says, and I think of my papa standing on the banks of a smallish river, or perhaps wading into the River Devon, and casting and casting, and casting again, watching the line sweep behind and round to fall into the water with a satisfying slap. When I'm on the train up from Glasgow, or driving the A9, I occasionally see fishers standing in the middle of the Tay, just before Pitlochry, or closer to home, on the Spey, and I always think of him, even after all this time.

Though my papa was a member of a fishing club, as far as

I know he usually went fishing on his own. He was a bus driver, and my mum said he hated driving a bus full of fishermen on trips and would avoid it at all costs. Though he was a chauffeur before the war, he never had his own car, and I don't remember ever seeing him behind the wheel of one. I wonder about him on his own, sitting on a bus for an hour or more, on his day off from being a bus driver and covering a lot of the same route he must sometimes have driven. He'd have had his lunch with him – his pieces all wrapped up (gammon or potted hough on slices of plain bread) and a flask of hot water. I have a small metal canister of his too, a thin, somewhat tarnished, silvery lozenge-shaped cylinder with a lid at each end, one side for sugar, the other for tea leaves.

Every fly has a name, apparently:

Teal and Green
Teal Blue and Silver
Mallard Claret
Cinnamon and Gold

And some are named after people:

a Kate McLaren
a Peter Ross
a Jock Scott

And I wonder if they are named after their inventors, to celebrate someone, or to appease long-suffering partners.

My papa's flies are all old and handmade, so they don't quite adhere to the names or their descriptions. Flies tend to be much more prefabricated and store-bought now, and sure enough, when I go onto a fly-fishing website I see that Cinnamon and Gold costs £1.04 for a pack of twelve. I can remember my papa in his shed, his big hands, rough with work and gardening, so dextrous in winding the fishing line around feathers and anything to hand that would work to make the flies. The same hands that would reach for my elbow and nip my funny bone, the same hands that would hold me on a bike as he taught me to ride, the same hands that, when he started to have dementia, would pull me into his bedroom to show me an imaginary staircase coming from the centre of the room that he'd point to and decry the bastards who were coming down to steal his things.

Maybe I just remember him bent over, peering, intent on fixing or making or repairing something or other that required every ounce of attention. My papa was always a maker, a tinkerer. He would go up to his shed and make his fishing flies, he'd fix people's wrist and pocket watches, and he'd pick up broken radios from the Barras. He'd sit at a fold-out table by the living-room window, with a single eye glass, and try to repair them. Later, as he got older and, probably, dementia began to kick in, he was unable to repair the watches and somewhere we have a bag of old pocket-watch cases and their inner workings, all mixed together. Cogs and wheels and the tiniest of screws.

When he came back from the war, Mum said he had the option to become either an undertaker or a bus driver, and chose the latter. She added that before the war, possibly just after he got married, he'd originally had an apprenticeship to be some kind of instrument maker but hadn't followed it through, or Gran didn't want him to – perhaps because he wouldn't have earned enough – and she wondered whether he might have been happier if he'd done it. I wonder about this now – whether her recollection of him is of someone who was fundamentally unhappy or discontent – and wish I'd asked more. I can't quite bring myself to ask. Through the visor of my childhood, I can remember no overriding emotions one way or the other – he was just there as my papa. He gave me a wee fishing rod and showed me how to cast, and I remember standing out on the path at the back door practising onto the back green, though I can't recall ever going fishing properly with him.

I don't know the trajectory of his life. I vaguely remember him coming in from his shift as a bus driver on the Midland route between Kilsyth and Glasgow, but I must have been young when he retired. I remember going with him down to the Castleview garden and how he'd set tripwires attached to shotgun shells that would fire off to dissuade wee boys from climbing into the garden to steal his fruit, and we'd sometimes trip them by mistake. He'd fill a barrel full of water so that boys jumping over the wall into the garden would land in it.

After he retired, he volunteered at the Cottage Hospital in Kilsyth, becoming their gardener. He used to ride his bike up and down to work, an old three-gear bike with a dynamo that would click onto the wheel and light the lamp at the front when the wheel was in motion. As I write this I can hear the sound of the dynamo, from its slow, low start to a high-pitched whirr that undulated as the wheels sped and slowed, but I must surely be remembering the sound of the dynamo on my own bike. The clock he was presented with when he retired used to hang on the wall in our living room, and my mum recently told me that gran didn't go to the retirement party the hospital threw for him. Frustratingly fragmented facts of lives lived.

And of my papa in his youth? Of his early life as the son of a blacksmith at the canal, and of growing up, school and after, I don't know that much. Before the Second World War he was a chauffeur and gardener for a family who owned an opticians, and who owned a 'big house' up in Dullatur – just east and on the other side of the canal from Auchinstarry. Some of gran's sisters were maids up there, and mum thinks that would be how he met my gran, but we don't know for sure.

We find a letter of reference for my papa with the stamp of Dullatur House embossed as a letterhead (and when I google Dullatur House, I come across an estate agent's video from when the house was on the market, and it's huge and still has a billiard room). The letter was written in 1941, when he was called up for war duty, and regrets the loss of his service, thanking him for his twenty-one years. My papa is described as 'a man of the highest integrity, absolutely trustworthy and of excellent character'. He must have started working there in around 1919, aged around sixteen or seventeen, and we wonder, if he left school at fourteen or so, what he did before he started there.

And somewhere, now lost, though it must have been so

precious, is a framed Certificate of Merit that my papa got from Rolls-Royce for the care and attention he gave to the car, and a Rolls-Royce Driver's Badge. We've still got the letter from Rolls-Royce mentioning both, but nothing more:

> As the Badge is only awarded to drivers who in our opinion maintain their cars in excellent order, we desire to draw your attention to the importance of safely guarding your Badge. If lost it is likely to get into the hands of a driver not entitled to it, thereby lowering the value of the badges in the possession of certificated drivers.

We've a fabled photograph of my papa in a kilt from this time, and the accompanying story is that the servants waited until the family were all out of the house and then dressed up in their finery, and I can't quite imagine him having that mischievousness, or our family being up so close to and aware of such class distinctions, and I wonder what they thought.

A HERON FLIES AROUND AND ABOUT the house sometimes. I'm presuming it's the same one, but I don't know for sure. It's been coming for quite some time now, and always alone. It perches on top of the electricity pole in the field and in one of the mature birches that stands in a clump just before the Scots pines start. Usually it flies down and lands in the middle of the small burn that in the summer trickles and, after an *evendoun*, or when in spate, or in the winter after a snow melt, becomes a torrent. Recently, it flew low into a spot with a patch of alders and birches; I know the burn is wider and shallower there, and it's one of the first places to look for celandine come spring. The burn is invisible from where I sit writing, though if I'm outside or the window is open, I can hear it to varying degrees. An alder grows on its bank, and for a year or so, after a new fence was put in with a convenient corner post to sit my camera on, I'd film it for twenty seconds or more. Sometimes I filmed daily, sometimes two or three times in a day if I was about and the light or weather changes intrigued.

Sometimes it was only once a week or two. I caught small birds landing and martins flying around it. Once, a buzzard landed just behind. A couple of times, some deer walked into the frame and out again. I tried to place the camera at exactly the same spot, with exactly the same focal length, but when I came to edit the clips together in sequence, there were some discrepancies, though, for the most part, they weren't too bad.

The finished film, that I called *aar*, a Scots word for alder, shows how the tree and its environs change season by season. Now, I look at the tree anew and wonder whether I've caught a particular light or wind or slant of sun, whether I should film it again. I've filmed it through the shifting times of the day, through the strength of the wind and rain, through the birds and animals and flowers that sometimes appear and disappear from the frame, and from that first, tentative growth in early spring to the fullness of high summer to the sparseness, the seeming hopelessness of what it becomes as the year draws to a close. The summer viridescence of the larches and birches beyond, shifting to autumn umbers, raw and burnt, and winter greens and purples, and the seeming constancy of the Scots pines. In the summer, swallows and martins swoop above and around it, following the course of the water to drink and look for insects. I've just watched a buzzard fly low past the tree and then up to alight on the same pole the heron lands on, flake down and levitate back up with a vole. The burn has a name which means 'the small dark one', and it flows to another, then another and finally out to sea.

dawn to dusk

scraigh-o' day	the first appearance of dawn
grey o' the morning	dawn of the day
greking	peep of day
day-sky	the appearance of the sky at break of day
lichtening	dawn
creek o' day	daybreak
dawing	dawn of day
scaud o' day	daybreak
morning-mun	increasing daylight
sky	the light at the eastern horizon before sunrise, or at the western after sunset; thus, 'was ye up afore the sin the day?' 'ay, afore the sky', or 'the sky winna set this hour yet'
between the sun and the sky	the interval between daybreak and sunrise

neb-o'-the-morning	the time between dawn and sunrise
morning-blink	early morning light
craw-day	dawn; the morning
midtime o' day	midday
between-the-lights	twilight
dayligaun	the twilight
day-sky	the appearance of the sky at break of day
gray	twilight
gloaming	twilight
gloaming-fa'	twilight, evening
gloam't	in the state of twilight
sockin-hour	the portion of time between daylight and candlelight
darkening	the evening, twilight
forenicht	the early part of the night; the interval between twilight and bedtime
between-the-lights	twilight
humin	twilight
day-sky	the appearance of the sky at twilight
neuk-time	the twilight; in reference to its being the season for pastime or gossiping among work-people
gloaming-shot	a twilight interval which workmen within doors take before using lights

nycht	to stop work for the day; to cease from labour when daylight closes
nichting-time	the time when outdoor labour ceases during the winter season, i.e., when daylight closes
forenicht	the early part of the night; the interval between twilight and bedtime
heel o' the twilight	the termination of twilight
nicht	night, the evening
nicht-come	nightfall
undern	the third hour of the artificial day, according to the ancient reckoning, i.e., nine o'clock
dim	midnight
the head of the dim	midsummer twilight between sunset and sunrise
nicht-mirk	the darkness of night

moor-burn   the annual burning of part of a moor; an
outbreak of temper; a dispute, conflict

fern-storm   rain caused by the burning of fern or heather

O<small>N PARTICULAR KINDS OF SPRING</small> or autumn days, you'll
be driving up the A9, and if you look over to the hillsides – say, over to the Monadhliath mountains or north to the
hills beyond Grantown, or the hills of any of the high moors
around – you'll often see tell-tale plumes of smoke drifting up
in thin ribbons before being dissipated by the wind. There are
days I associate with seeing such things. If it's spring, you'll still
be able to see patches of snow on the peaks and in some of
the shaded hollows in the hills, and you'll feel the beginnings
of some heat to the sun. If September, there's the weakening
of its strength associated with the turn of the season. The day
will be still, or will come with a slight breeze and blue skies,
maybe with cirrus higher up, or cumulus at its edges. If spring,

I expect to hear and then see ragged skeins of geese in the sky above; if autumn, I look up with an expectation of their arrival.

Muirburning, nowadays sometimes called 'prescribed burning', involves the burning of areas of moorland and the grasses and heather therein. That's what we see on these distant hills. Burning releases nutrients, and the new growth provides better and more varied food sources. Nethersole-Thompson and Watson observed: 'Burning, to remove rank vegetation, became standard practice in the nineteenth century. This muirburn has prevented regeneration of scrub and forest and led to fewer kinds of plants. Shepherds, deer stalkers and gamekeepers burn moors to provide a "young bite" for sheep, deer and grouse.'[67] These days, debates rage about the purpose and extent of this practice, and, increasingly, the implications of burning for releasing carbon into the atmosphere, and how important the peatlands are for carbon storage. There are further fears not just about the carbon that is released into the atmosphere during burns, but how the remaining peat, so vital for carbon storage, can be degraded and how that in turn affects drainage and water quality as well as the biodiversity and long-term ecological health of these places.

Some have argued that fire can be seen as one of the earliest ways in which land has been managed. Fire – think of lightning strikes – has always been a regular, natural changer of environments, but it's sometimes an unnatural changer of environments too. We've seen in recent years how fire has taken lives and devastated unfathomably massive areas of the Amazon, the US,

Australia, South Africa, Siberia and elsewhere, sometimes started by lightning, arson, a stray cigarette or campfires or muirburns that have gone out of control.

In 2021, an area of Table Mountain in South Africa I'd visited in 2020 was partly devastated by a wildfire thought to have been started by arson. This region is home to a kind of vegetation known as the fynbos biome – a unique floral ecosystem that holds many shrub-like plants. It is a place that includes some of the most concentrated areas of endemic and endangered plants in the world. In the fynbos biome, there are over 600 ericas (heathers and heaths), as well as countless species and subspecies of pincushions, sugarbushes, irises and orchids and other fine-leaved shrubby plants. Fire (of the right kind, in the right season) for many of these plants isn't an option but necessary for their regeneration. They're described as being pyrophytes – fire-loving – and many need fire for germination through either heat or smoke, as well as the minerals found in the ash.[68] Without fire, these short-lived fynbos species are taken over by other thicket species, and will wither and die, and wait, dormant, for the next fire to come along and restart their growing cycle, start their successional clock ticking once more. Just outside Cape Town, an ecologist showed me around an area that had been gutted by fire just over a decade ago and talked about their surprise at the rare species that had grown out of the devastation – species that had lain dormant for a century. 'After fire, first one kind of plant – say, the orchid – grows, then after a year or two the ericas, then after, the pincushions, then, after fifteen years it all goes downhill and it's ready to burn again.' Still, it's one thing for the good of the plants, another for the good of the general environment, or when it burns in close proximity to, and sometimes too close to, populations. Climate change may bring altogether different kinds of fires and associated precarities. The 2021 Table Mountain fire threatened lives and livelihoods, and destroyed property that included a library at the university that housed many important artefacts and archives relating to the history of South Africa.

I've only been close to fire in this way once, over a decade ago, when the RSPB carried out a small, controlled burn as part of their land management plan at that time, to protect a rare population of bearberry heath on the edge of a forest that was in danger of being overwhelmed by heather. It's not something they do now, preferring to monitor the bearberry population and explore other options for its protection. But that day is another of these moments that stay with me, not least for how it made me aware of how vulnerable my proximity to fire made me feel.

It started with one of the rangers using a drip torch, a metal canister with a loop in its neck, to set lines of the land alight. The petrol trickled out, dribbled onto the ground and was ignited. As the ranger walked with the liquid flames behind him, he created a line of fire that was then carried forward by the breeze. We stood ready to beat the lead fires in case they began to burn too ferociously. Others stood at its edges, ready to stop it from spreading over more ground than we could manage to handle. Prior to this, a barrier of scorched earth was established at the end where the breeze would carry the flame, creating a fire break that the flames, should they reach it, would not leap over. A tractor with tank and water cannon was always on stand-by.

It felt so counterintuitive moving towards the flames when one's instinct was to back away. The beaters were heavy in our hands, and their rubberised ends carried their own momentum. I wore a skip cap to shield my eyes and protect my hair, and natural, non-meltable materials under a fireproof jacket and overalls. We were close enough to see how the flames caught and ripped, hear the roar and hiss, and, like a bonfire on a cold evening, feel, on this cobalt-blue spring morning, while our backs were cold, the heat of the flames on our faces which made us flinch and blink.

We stood in lines behind or to the side of the burn and waited for it to reach us, ready to beat it out, watching for any stray embers. The heat burned, dried eyes and cheeks. A liquid haze of silhouetted beaters was visible on the other side of the flames. Shadows lengthened through the smoke, and it thickened and thinned from blue-grey to yellow to white, and when the wind shifted and flurried, suddenly, momentarily, we'd be engulfed with smoke. And the sound, a constant noise, visceral, kept us leery, the hiss and crackle louder when dryer vegetation caught alight, and a deeper rumble as the flames enfolded and engulfed even as it moved on, and something tells you that you should not be walking towards it, or even holding your ground, but backing away, yet we had to stand firm and sometimes move closer to help beat out the flames. Being so close, it was easy to see how quickly a fire might get out of control: a sudden gust whipping an ember, unobserved, that would lie smouldering and biding its time; a change in wind direction momentarily blinding us with smoke and sending flames in an unexpected direction.

There's been fire, and a fear of fire, in Abernethy for centuries, and records reveal natural and unnatural fires that have changed the structure of the forest. Steven and Carlisle report: 'In 1693, burning heather too close to the pinewoods rendered the culprit liable to be nailed to the gallows with a ten-penny nail through the ear.' The Reverend W. Forsyth also talked about a fire in 1746: 'The tradition as to this fire is, that a certain smith who had his forge at the verge of the forest was complaining one day of the trouble he had with horses that went astray in the dense woods. A Lochaber man who heard him said, "*Make me a good dirk* [a kind of dagger]*, and I'll take in hand to save you from such trouble.*" He agreed. Next day the forest was in a blaze, and a wide clearance was soon made. The Cameron disappeared for a twelvemonth, but then he came quietly and claimed his dirk.'[69] In 1762, an article about Abernethy in the *Aberdeen Journal* spoke of a fire that had encompassed much of the woods and endangered many lives: 'The unwarrantable practice of heath or moor-burning, at all times dangerous, but much more so during such a long continued drought, has lately been attended with very disagreeable consequences ... the woods of Abernethy have suffered prodigiously, and all the neighbouring inhabitants were for several days and nights employed in diverting the course, or extinguishing the flames.'[70] Reverend W. Forsyth refers to the 1770 conflagration, which required 500 men to extinguish it.

More recently, and I mean just over a century ago, the *Strathspey Herald* reported a fire that swept from Nethy Bridge to Tulloch and then Loch Garten, and in Ron Summers' book on Abernethy, the images around Loch Garten, taken in 1928, are remarkable for the lack of trees. Nan Shepherd talks about the fire of 1920 in nearby Rothiemurchus Forest: 'One of the gamekeepers told me that forty of them were on the watch for ten days and nights to keep the fire from spreading. And by night, he said, the tree trunks glowed like pillars of fire.'[71] Summers reports more recent, smaller fires too, and concerns about fire aren't relegated to the past. Even today, if there's been a dry spell, signs go up warning of fire danger and instructing people not to light fires, and there's a local WhatsApp group to alert each other and the authorities if we see anything untoward.

It can feel that these woods are timeless, and – in this era where there's been a shift from timber to sport and conservation – that they'll be safe and protected and secure. But within them, from the smallest microhabitat, each tree and the forest itself, like any living thing, is vulnerable. Ron Summers: 'It is notable too that the amount of rainfall in June 1920 at Nethy Bridge was the joint lowest on record. The dry conditions would certainly have helped the fire spread.'[72] Who knows what changes in climate might bring? How might alterations in mean temperature and rainfall change the habitat and its suitability for species? What might come in and what might go? What might these woods themselves decide to do?

I'D NEVER REALLY THOUGHT TO look at moths until one day in a warm July. They are quiet and unobtrusive, invisibly going about their business hidden by night, and day moths flit past like tiny, burnt fragments of paper caught in a breeze. An adult moth, I discovered, is called an imago, and the plural is imagines (though imagoes is also acceptable). According to NatureScot, over 1,300 species of moths have been recorded in Scotland,[73] and they are another important element of Scotland's biodiversity. Blue tit chicks alone are estimated to feed on 35 billion caterpillars every year in the UK.[74] In the course of the twentieth century, five species of butterfly and over sixty species of moth have become extinct, because of, amongst other things, habitat loss or fragmentation, pollution, changes in agriculture and forestry, or changes in climate.[75, 76] It makes sense that their sensitivity to the changing environment makes them invaluable in helping gauge the health of the environment. Now, I notice more of them and I'm much more attuned to their presence, but they are so flighty that I can rarely identify them. Tiny black chimney moths, their sooty wings rimmed with white, appear in the time just after the pignuts blossom, and in midsummer countless geometrids pepper the forest, their caterpillars an important food source for capercaillies. Late March one year, we had a week of Hebrew characters, pine beauties, common quakers and clouded drabs knocking on the windows, along with the Rannoch sprawler. In the summer when the bladder campion blooms, eight or nine long-tongued moths of a kind I've not yet quite been able to identify cluster around the white flowers, delving into their calyx.

That first July, a nature tour guide came by the friends' house in Abernethy where I was staying and asked if he could put a moth trap at the bottom of the garden just inside the forest, in order to catch some of the pinewood species of moths. He set it up and left, and I turned it on when it started to get dark.

A moth trap is a contraption that sits in the woods like an alien thing. When it's switched on, it seems to lure every night-time flying insect towards it, and it casts a light on the surrounding leaves and bracken that makes the greens even brighter than in the midday sun, creating a space of seeing and knownness that makes, somehow, the surrounding space feel darker.

When I stood at the edges of the light, facing in, I could feel the darkness press upon me, and the eeriness and uncanniness of night at my back. Turning away from the glare, despite the midsummer dim, all was black.

The moths came, as if to a flame, and when I went close and listened over the breeze that rustled the bracken I could hear their wings as they hit the light. Sometimes they flew below it and into the chamber, where, with only a small chance they'd get back out, they flittered and rested, flittered and rested on the empty egg cartons that had been placed inside.

Many species of moth were first identified in the Victorian era by amateur naturalists, and their names are strange, romantic, evocative, and, like those of pedigree dogs or racehorses, somehow don't always sound like names.

mottled beauty
marbled carpet
lesser swallow prominent
common white wave
pale shouldered brocade
true lover's knot
birch mocha
willow beauty
poplar hawkmoth
coxcomb prominent
common lutestring
bordered white
dingy skipper
sallow kitten
ghost moth
green arches

I watched and filmed the trap, watching the micro- and macro-moths arrive and gather and swirl above the light, occasionally falling in, and left when the midges arrived. In the morning, when the guide came back and opened the trap to lift out the egg boxes to show his group of holidaymakers what the forest had offered up, the moths sat rigor-still for inspection, like those in museum entomology collections that are long dead and have been caught and pinned, categorised, compartmentalised and boxed away. The guide gently picked them up to study them more closely and, after naming them, set them down once more to become leaves, bracken or flakes of bark.

EVERY CHRISTMAS MY PARTNER AND I go home to Kilsyth to spend it with my mum, and every Christmas Day we go up to my aunt and uncle's farmhouse, just above the town and into the hills. Assorted cousins and their kids all descend, and we'll invariably talk about people and the town, and childhood memories, and laugh incredulously at what some of the teachers at the school were like, or the dentist we had in primary school, who we now call 'the butcher of Kilsyth'. (He gave everyone a full set of fillings, whether, we reckon now, we needed them or not.) Every Christmas morning, my partner and I go for a walk, taking a path through the new houses that now populate the Couches to the Stirling Road and heading around the dam and up to Colzium through the bluebell wood to the Tak Ma Doon Road, up to the High Line and home. We'll do the same on Boxing Day, perhaps going for a wee bit longer and leaving my mum at home to give her some peace. One year, the year of a large irruption, on our way back from the canal just before we headed back home via Mal Fleemin's Brae, we heard the sound of tiny bells and followed the noise to see the gift of four or five waxwings on the top of a birch tree. For the last couple of years, my cousin, who stays in her paternal grandparents' house just down the road from my mum's, has come walking too, and we've ended up in the pub that sits on the canal at Auchinstarry, which must be across from where the bridgekeeper's house and the smiddy used to be, where our grandfather stayed as a boy.

When I look up over the hills from my mum's living room, trees now peek over the ridge from the Forestry Commission forests that grow on the northern side of the hills, towards the Carron Reservoir and Stirling, along the back road to Fintry, jagging the horizon. We can also see the scars from where there used to be trees that have now been harvested and the patches of new planting, and a new track up across a field to the west of the glen that my mum thinks goes up to Johnnie's dam and may or may not be something to do with hydro-electric power.

I remember my papa telling me that when the sheep were high up on the hills we'd have good weather and when they came down from the hills the weather was going to change, but I don't know if that's true or not, and I can't recall seeing many sheep there in recent years.

I've friends from school who've moved away and whose families have moved away, or whose parents have died and they've not been back to Kilsyth for years, having no reason to come back, and I can't quite imagine when I will no longer have the muscle memory of return.

bide   to wait, to wait for; to wait for, as implying the idea
of defiance; to suffer, to endure

IN 2020, BECAUSE OF LOCKDOWN, I was able to work at home
for an extended period, spring to summer to winter to spring
and back to summer. My walks were local, repeated, with only
very occasional forays further afield when restrictions allowed
– usually to visit my mum. I felt so insular, vulnerable yet protected
from the world. Though I missed my mum and it felt strange to
have the ability to go home to Kilsyth taken away, every morning
I opened the blinds and the days looked so normal. I noticed
the first buds on the larches and alders; waited for and watched
the swallows and the martins return; saw the thin dusting of
pollen from the Scots pines cover every surface, inside and out,
at the very end of each May; and saw young swallows fledge and
sit quivering at first, like novice tightrope walkers, on the electricity wires outside the house. Then they left, 'ours' first, then
others came and went in dribs and drabs right through October.

That year, I heard my first willow warbler on the 17th of April and my first cuckoo of the year on the 24th, the very day my neighbour, who's lived here far longer than we have, predicted they'd return. From 2021, I've a note questioning whether I heard a willow warbler's song on the 14th – earlier than some years – and I remember it because I heard its falling cadence just the once, and it had finished by the time my brain caught up to what my ears thought they'd heard. I began to hear them more regularly from the 20th, and I heard my first cuckoo of the year on the 28th. By the time be*longing* is published, summer and winter visitors will have returned, left again and returned, and some will be thinking about leaving, others of returning, and I will have noted the dates of these comings and goings once more.

In 2020, my understanding of duration altered, and in these old Scots language dictionaries that I keep returning to, I found those words and phrases for the nuances of light and how a northern thread of it lingers from the end of one day to the beginning of the next, at *the head of the dim*, midsummer twilight between sunset and sunrise.

As the days lengthened, roe deer would hover at the edges of the field in the evening, close to the bracken and junipers and the woods behind. Occasionally, they were joined by red deer. We watched the woodcock ride above the trees in geometric lines as we waited for the hares to appear. These things happen every year; I just had more time to see and note them in that space of lockdown.

In the time before the flick of a light switch, there was a

gentler easing into the night, and when time stretches beyond the hours of the day to months of the year, so many of the words and descriptions in these old dictionaries are rooted in nature and the land. March's *craw-Sunday*, April's *gowk-storm*, July's *worm month*. And then, at the far end of the summer, the *breakback moon*, *stooky Sunday*, *go-harvest*, *lang halter time*, through to the *deid time o' the year* – midwinter, when there is no vegetation.

Knowledge of forthcoming weather was rooted in experience and what was visible, and usually in the soon to be, the near present: *heavy-heartit clouds* threatening rain; a *gow*, a halo round the sun or moon portending bad weather. Even other phrases that are longer in term refer to near-predictable Scottish weather events: *May-gobs*, cold weather in May; a *Lammas-flood*, heavy rain around August.[77]

We've always reached to nature and the earth for alignment, solace, comparison. I come across phases like *neb-o'-the-mire-snipe*, meaning the utmost extremity, and *cheepart*, a meadow pipit, or a small person with a shrill voice. *Drizzen* means to low as a cow or ox, and is sometimes applied to a sluggard groaning over his work. A *ferny-buss* is a clump of ferns, but it's used in the phrase 'it's either a tod [fox] or a ferny-buss', meaning it's something or other, no matter what. *To peak* means to chirp or to squeak but also to speak in a whisper or thin, weak voice or to complain of poverty. As a noun, it means the chirp of a bird, the squeak of a mouse, an insignificant voice, a small person with a thin, weak voice. I've loved the phrase *to spurrie-how*, to run as fast as a sparrowhawk flies, since I found it. It speaks again of that first reach of metaphor to what is known and what is seen and imagined.

I listened to a podcast recently where they described how weather forecasting as we know it today came about at the time of the invention of the telegraph, when news and the sharing of information could move faster than clouds, and we could become one step ahead.[78] Now, I have an app on my phone which tells me that it will start raining here in three minutes and end thirty-five minutes later, and nature is not necessarily our first port of call. Now, we measure upload speeds and download speeds in terms of milliseconds, and we can travel around the world or be connected and alerted to actions and atrocities and movements and thinking in ways which were unimaginable mere decades ago. We can think of speed and time in terms of light years and, perhaps, long nows.[79] On a daily basis we're asked to think in abstracts and what-ifs in speeds and times beyond the human scale, and while Covid brought extraordinary stress and anxiety and worry, for me it was also good to see what it is to be this sedentary, to slow to this pace of walking even while recognising our vulnerability, our vincibility and what we take for granted.

We've seen how Steven and Carlisle talk about these pine-woods, noting that 'the surviving native pine-woods are the lineal descendants of early post-glacial times', and that 'even to walk through the larger of them gives one a better idea of what a primeval forest was like'. These forests, or forests like them, if not exactly as they were, or exactly where they are now, were in existence when wolves and lynx still roamed the country. The granny pine that still stands, carved with a 'B', and from which fir candles were cut, would just have been a young thing when slavery was abolished.

From the eighteenth century, we've had an awareness of deep time and have looked beyond our present existence to a geological scale that measures time and change in millions of years. A couple of hours' drive northwest from where I stay lies Sutherland and the Knockan Crag. It sits within and over-looks Norman MacCaig's favoured landscape, one of mine too. He writes of this area in his poem, 'A Man in Assynt':

> Glaciers, grinding West, gouged out
> these valleys, rasping the brown sandstone,
> and left, on the hard rock below –
> the ruffled foreland –
> this frieze of mountains, filed
> on the blue air

Knockan Crag is said to be one of the first important sites of modern geology, and it's a place where it's easy to see the Moine Thrust, where two continents crashed together and older rock pushed and crushed and folded and rested on top of younger rocks, disrupting layers of time. 'At Knockan Crag,' the Tourist Board tells us, 'you can bridge 500 million years of history with your bare hands.'

Now, we're told we're living in the Anthropocene, and we're still thinking of it in terms of decades and centuries, not in the millions of geological years by which such 'cenes are usually measured. It's a strange thing to have to think about our own responsibilities within a continuing timespan of earth that's hitherto been rooted in the slow formation of rocks and changes in climate that have had nothing to do with humanity. We're adding plastic and carbon and radioactive isotopes to layers of time that have been seen and shown in rock strata. Now, there are interconnections to rock and minerals and how we've used this earth, and they're present in histories and projections of future times near and far that are written and being rewritten as I write.

In these past couple of years everything has felt strange, increasingly precarious. Beyond the world of politics and the more day-to-day stuff of life we have perpetual fears and worries about the effects of climate change and Covid on everyone and everything on earth and how, generally, we live in the world. So much from March 2020 to summer 2021 and beyond felt reduced to the day-to-day, the immediate, the local, though at the same time I looked out across the world in ways that our forebears would never have thought possible. I read about carbon emissions falling because of the reduction in travel by air, land and sea. I watched with horror the murder of George Floyd and the subsequent protests against racism and police brutality. I saw long-standing monuments to racists – the slave owner Edward Colston in Bristol, the Confederate General Robert E. Lee in the US – being pulled down. I watched the bounce-back too. I witnessed the end of Trump's presidency and, in disbelief, the UK's exit from Europe, and experienced the immediate ramifications. I saw Covid vaccines approved, took note of how effective they seemed to be, and was lucky enough to be able to take advantage of their availability. At the end of 2021 COP26 came to Glasgow and around the world people took to the streets to convey their fears about climate change and to demand swift action. I also witnessed the horrific and evolving impact of Covid and its variants as the numbers in the UK and elsewhere fell, then climbed, then fell and climbed again, saw inequities in how Covid vaccines were available and rolled out across the world, and sensed that any return to normality would be tinged with danger and fragility. In other parts of the world, wars and conflicts simmered and escalated, and carbon emissions began to rise once more.

The Doomsday Clock is a commentary/metaphor about the existential threats to human life that started in the 1950s. Then, it related to the threat of nuclear proliferation to the world; now, it considers the climate emergency and changes and developments in technology – and it seems to creep ever closer to midnight.[80] It's been close before: with nuclear capability and testing during the Cold War and other international crises it was sometimes at two or three minutes to midnight. I remember the humming late-night fear of nuclear war when I was a teenager, going to CND marches in Glasgow, and being so conscious of the nuclear arsenal housed only forty miles northwest of Glasgow at Faslane – a place we could just about see from some of our school hillwalking club trips to the Arrochar Alps. Somewhere in Kilsyth, I'm sure I have an old CND *Protest and Survive* leaflet and my copy of Raymond Briggs' *When the Wind Blows* – the graphic novel published in

1982 that was a terrifying, poignant depiction of nuclear war seen through the eyes of an elderly couple. These things we live in fear of that we don't feel we can control. In 1995, the Doomsday Clock crept back to fourteen minutes to midnight, but it's more or less been ticking down since then. In 2021, it was set at 100 seconds to midnight.[81]

How can we understand the ways in which the past impacts on our sense of the present and, thereafter, our possible futures? Scotland and its long and short, natural and unnatural histories and the transformation of its people and land have been surveyed in non-fiction, fiction, poetry and song, and the complexities of the Clearances, Scotland's role in the British Empire and the involvement of its people in colonisation, subjugation and slavery have been written about by many far more knowledge-able than me.

We're in the Anthropocene, and these trees, or their ante-cedents, existed before this era; now, they are living through it and all it holds. Discussions about when the Anthropocene starts complicate and implicate in different ways. Some have argued that the Anthropocene really began in the middle of the twentieth century, with the detonation of the first atomic bombs and the radioactivity cast up into the atmosphere from the 1950s. Some have pinpointed the start of it to the time of Columbus and into the sixteenth century, with the beginnings of the exchange of species between the 'Old' and 'New' Worlds, and others have argued that it started at the advent of the Industrial Revolution.[82, 83] Steven and Carlisle describe how at the beginning of the commercial exploitation of the forest, the trees became ships, became masts, became water pipes (and how, then, might these trees be implicated in the spread of 'empire'?) until it became uneconomical again, and timber made way for 'sport'.

T.C. Smout, writing about the social history of Scotland and 'material wellbeing' noted that 'to the economic historian there is a triumphal progression down to the First World War: the success of the first phase of the industrial revolution is succeeded by the success of iron and coal in the second, then after 1860 by the triumph of steel, ships, jute, tweed and high farming . . . to the social historian – or at least to me – things seem rather different.' He writes – and these early years are when the Jamieson dictionary (1846) was compiled – 'the age of great industrial triumphs was an age of appalling social deprivation'.[84] I reflect again on the end of the timber years at Abernethy: the abandoned settlements and the 104 people displaced in the late 1800s; the miners' row at the Haggs; my great-uncles as miners; my gran's siblings in service as maids in a 'big house'; and their father as a labourer, foundry worker, miner – depending on which of his children's birth certificates you look at.

Smout draws attention to the impact of the Industrial Revolution on Scotland's working folk, but Kathryn Yusoff,[85] Professor of Inhuman Geography (and what a great job title that is) at the Queen Mary University of London, adds more, revealing the seam of colour running through the Anthropocene. She's interested in changing what she calls the 'grammar' and 'language' of geology, adding another corporeality and responsibility to it. If the Anthropocene started with Columbus (or

AMANDA THOMSON

thereabouts) and the beginning of the trade and the movement of species between Europe and the Americas then, '"the collision of the old and new" covers over the friction of a less smooth, more corporeal set of racialized violences'. These are exchanges which are 'the directed colonial violence of forced eviction from land, enslavement on plantations, in rubber factories and mines, and the indirect violence of pathogens through forced contact and rape . . .'.[86] Of the Industrial Revolution, Yusoff writes: 'In 1833, Parliament finally abolished slavery in the British Caribbean, and the taxpayer payout of £20 million in "compensation" [to slave owners!] built the material, geophysical (railways, mines, factories), and imperial infrastructure of Britain and its colonial enterprises and empire'.[87] If it started with atomic testing, then 'nuclear testing marks the displacement and exposure of indigenous peoples in the Pacific Islands and the radiation of Native American and Aboriginal peoples in North America and Australia'.[88] She writes that 'the end of this world has already happened for some subjects, and it is the prerequisite for the possibilities of imagining "living and breathing again" for others'.[89]

The pandemic and the increasing effects of climate change seem to further expose these deep-rooted inequities. During lockdown, some of us were lucky and could sit in our domestic bubbles, thankful to be home and in a home that felt safe, wondering and worrying about how much of what has happened has changed minds or will force change. How many of us felt, and still feel, that quiver of powerlessness and limitation that we've always felt in the world, overwhelmed by catastrophic failures to value human life, in that same way that we can't quite comprehend the vastness of deep time or the complications of what needs to be done to make things better? Or the massive scale and resetting of our ways of being that the correction to our trajectory as it stands, needs?

Eard-din is an old Scots word meaning 'thunder, thunder in the earth, an earthquake', and I can only think that it's a composite word meaning earth noise – a fascinating conflation of air and land, air and rock. How easy it is up here, out walking, to quiet the noise, to drown out that which I don't want to hear. It can take all our strength to listen to and understand and find a way to act on what we are hearing. Sometimes it's all we can do just to be here. There's another old phrase I return to often and wonder whereabouts we are, literally and metaphorically: *a hearkenin' win'* – 'a comparative lull in a storm, followed by a destructive blast'.

PART III

PART III

For years, on our family Sunday walks when we walked along the canal, we'd have gone past where my papa and his father and grandfather stayed. I wonder what he thought in these moments. My recollection of the stories he'd tell, if any, are vague, and probably in that way when we're young and old people talk about their memories, we only half listen and disregard them until it's too late to ask any more. Once, when I was a child, someone from the Forth and Clyde Canal Society came to the house to interview my papa about his time at Auchinstarry, and though we couldn't find the series of booklets about the history of the canal that he was included in, I was able to track down Paul, the man who'd interviewed him. In that smalltown way, my mum was able to remember his name, and he still stays in Banton, the village at the head of the dam. A bit of me hoped that he would have an old tape recording of the interview, or something more tangible that would connect me to my papa, pull me in more. He kindly sent me a postcard of Auchinstarry from around 1900, with the bridge-keeper's cottage on the far right, where we reckon my papa and his family must have stayed, and a transcript of the interview:

In those days it was a bascule bridge, which we wound up and down by hand. It was replaced by a swing bridge just before the war. I well remember the horse-drawn scows taking pig iron from the Bonnybridge foundries to Glasgow. We had a loading bay by the bridge where coal and whinstone was loaded into scows from the local mines and quarries. A horse could pull a fifty-ton load, even if it did have a bit of difficulty getting started.

Working the bridge was easy as it was well balanced and I could manage it as a boy. My father's main work was in the smithy, shoeing canal horses and repairing miner's picks. When a boat approached, one of his dogs, Peggy or Nettle, would rush in barking to let him know. Several boats would pass in an hour and even in the night. The boatman would kick at the door at night to wake us up. One thing though, we got 2d a time for opening the bridge between 10 p.m. and 6 a.m.

It was a fine sight seeing the Leith boats going through, with white rings round their funnels, and the *Afghan*, a big steam boat. The fishing boats always caused a stir as they stopped at each village to sell their herring. The women came running down the hill with their pails for them. Some of the scows had a bit of time getting round the De'ils Elbow and Strone Point.

Sometimes they ran aground and waited for a steamer to pull them off.

We always had trouble with folk falling in the water, mostly drunks or boys who'd tried balancing on the handrails. My father used to haul them out with a hook on the end of a long pole. A favourite sport for the local kids was running along the towpath beside the *Gypsy Queen* to collect coppers thrown out by the passengers. They were good days then, down on the canal.

Yet, though these are my papa's words, his stories, I don't really remember him telling them to me. I can't hear the timbre of his voice or intonation, or remember the sound of how he laughed.

flouncing (use of trees in a gale), tossing to and fro

On some mornings, if I'm out, I can hear the distant, deep *pruuk* of ravens. I listen as the sound gets louder. They're often flying over from the east, seemingly out of the sun, and they fly high and over in ones and twos, and I've no idea where they've come from, or where they are going, and just as quickly as they appear, they're gone.

WHEN THE SWALLOWS COME, THEY come. One day there are none, and the next perhaps a couple or a group flying high and over, and then they're about the burn and on the wires – house martins too – and then they're omnipresent for the next few months. This year, the house martins came a day or two later, followed by the other summer visitors too – warblers, cuckoos, redstarts and ospreys, briefly, but they didn't linger. Suddenly, spring turned to summer, and the swallows were twittering and swooping and swirling about the field and dipping down to feed in the burn, building and rebuilding their nests in our neighbour's eaves. They stay all summer here, in Scotland and throughout Europe, then, as autumn falls, they leave. Until about 100 years ago, no one quite knew where swallows disappeared to, come the end of the summer, though conjecture wasn't as fanciful as in previous times:

Some naturalists suppose, that they do not leave this island
at the end of autumn, but that they lie in a torpid state,

till the beginning of summer, in the banks of rivers, in the hollows of decayed trees, in holes and crevices of old buildings, in sand banks, and the like: Some have even asserted, that swallows pass the winter immersed in the waters of lakes and rivers, where they have been found in clusters, mouth to mouth, wing to wing, foot to foot, and that they retire to these places in autumn, and creep down the reeds to their subaqueous retreats.[90]

In May 1911, at the birth of bird ringing in the UK, a metal ring with the number B830 was placed on the leg of a swallow caught in Staffordshire, England. The bird was found, in December 1912, in Natal, South Africa, giving us definitive proof of their long, unfathomable migrations.[91]

Given the size of these small, fluttering birds – they weigh around 18g on average, the weight of two five-rand or two £1 coins – that journey must have seemed as implausible as their supposed winter sojourns at the bottom of rivers. Now, we know more about them: they travel around 200 miles a day, resting at the same stopover points on their routes, flying low, eating insects along the way, and arriving wherever they are going six to eight weeks after they depart.[92]

Their migration has been tracked, and the easy arrows that cut the equator north to south on borderless maps of the world show the vast distances that these tiny birds cross, but hide the multiple perils they face.

Really, it was the swallows that sent me to South Africa. When I was approached to be part of the Edinburgh International

Book Festival's Outriders Africa project and asked where I might want to go, the swallows were arriving back in Scotland after their winter sojourns in the south, and I had been thinking about where they'd come from, the precarity of their journeys, the necessity of their migration. *Zughunruhe*, the migratory urge, made me wonder about where we think of as home, if we continually migrate between places. We call swallows summer visitors, geese and bramblings winter visitors, but surely they must feel at home wherever they are?

I arrived in Cape Town at the end of February 2020, welcomed by officials in face masks who checked the temperature of everyone coming through passport control. The world was beginning to feel increasingly unstable as the coronavirus started its spread around the world. It was hitting the news enough for me to be aware but was still distant enough in that way that events touch you but only quietly, and you have abstract, if empathic, concern. The temperature check and the one or two people who wore face masks on the plane brought it closer.

On the drive in from the airport I saw my first swallows of the year, months before I ordinarily would in Scotland. Soaring in the shimmering heat and against the cerulean sky of a late Capetonian summer, there they were, up and around the trees and buildings, resting on the telephone wires and poles, like they'd never been anywhere else, like they'd always be here.

I was there to spend time with the South African National Biodiversity Institute (SANBI), to learn more about the fynbos biome. To quote UNESCO: 'The Cape Floral Region is one of the richest areas for plants when compared to any similar sized area in the world. It represents less than 0.5% of the area of Africa but is home to nearly 20% of the continent's flora. The outstanding diversity, density and endemism of the flora are among the highest worldwide. Some 69% of the estimated 9,000 plant species in the region are endemic, with 1,736 plant species identified as threatened and with 3,087 species of conservation concern. The Cape Floral Region has been identified as one of the world's top biodiversity hotspots.'[93] Around 7% of the world's plants occur in South Africa – and 65% of them are endemic to the Cape Floral Region – that is, they occur nowhere else on earth. That's 7% of all plant species in the world in less than 2% of the land surface.[94] Nearly one quarter of this flora is either of concern or threatened with extinction.

SANBI is part of a worldwide partnership of agencies that form the Millennium Seed Bank Partnership (MSBP), and part of their remit is to gather seeds for this project. The MSBP focuses on gathering the seeds of plants that are under threat of extinction and plants which will be of most use in the future, and I spent much of my week looking for and collecting the seeds of some of the fynbos plants that sit in these categories. At the Royal Botanic Gardens in Kew, just outside London, there is, indeed, a bank – actually a flood-, bomb- and radiation-proof deep freeze – that holds seeds from around the world, including those of the rarest and most threatened of plants. It is a safety net for the future. For the past few years, a neighbour of mine has gathered Scots pine seeds for the MSBP, and I don't know if it's reassuring or deeply strange to think of there being (or needing to be) a central bank that keeps seeds from species across the globe for safekeeping.

When I was in Cape Town, I spent time with Victoria Wilman and her team at SANBI, who are based at Kirstenbosch National Botanical Garden, collecting seeds and learning about the work they do as part of the MSBP. I read: 'An extinct species is lost forever. Many species have cultural, medicinal and aesthetic value, and many support other species, such as parasites, predators and symbionts. Some species are keystone species and maintain entire food webs . . . species have a right to exist, just as much as we have a right to exist – this is called "intrinsic value"'.[95] Sometimes we don't yet know the value that a plant may have, or what forms that value might take. I think about the intrinsic value of dead wood.

At Kirstenbosch there's an area called 'the Garden of Extinction'. It contains examples of some of these threatened, endangered and vulnerable plants, and there are plaques to those already lost.

The **Whorled Heath** once grew on the Cape Flats but was wiped out by urban development, farming and flower picking.

ERICACEAE (HEATH FAMILY)
Erica verticillata 'Cherise'

EXTINCT IN THE WILD
CAPE FLATS SAND FYNBOS

Occasionally there's a kernel of hope.

> The last known wild population of the
> rare **Anemone Vygie** was destroyed in
> 1992, but it's possible that wild plants
> still exist.
>
> AIZOACEAE
> (VYGIE OR MESEMB FAMILY)
> **Jordaaniella anemoniflora**
>
> **CRITICALLY ENDANGERED
> (POSSIBLY EXTINCT)**

The first day out in the field, we drove up a steep red track that zigzagged up the back of Table Mountain, sometimes at angles so acute that the two trucks had to shoot beyond the tracks and curve around a circular turning point before the next rise. We were on a search for the *Disa uniflora* – an iconic Table Mountain/Western Cape species – and whatever else we might find along the way. This red disa, a single orchid, was known to grow at an aqueduct we were making our way towards. We walked along a thin, stony path that the fynbos spilled over and on to. It was thirty degrees and I was less than a week away from Scotland's frosts and blizzards, and in the barely remembered heat I felt the sweat prick my pores; my face was awash and dripping, and I wondered if I'd brought enough water with me. The fynbos, at that time of year, at the cusp of autumn, gave only occasional dots of other colours among the lushness and succulence of its greens and the blue, blue sky. Far below us was the sprawl of Cape Town, softened by an early morning haze that might have been the morning light or pollution or smoke from wildfires burning on the Stellenbosch Mountain beyond, and was probably a mixture of all three.

It was the kind of place I'd expect eagles to appear, or vultures, though I didn't even know if they were found there. A raven with a patch of white on its nape, and crows – pied crows, I believe – flew past, and I thought that despite how much was different, we always seek familiarity or start off with what is familiar in order to make sense of difference. I saw endless variations of heathers, the *ericas,* but rather than the purples of Scottish hillsides in autumn, these flowers were in whites, pinks, purples, yellows. Some had flowers with whorls of long, narrow, curved tubes that perfectly sheathed the bills of the iridescent sunbirds that occasionally flitted among them. I recognised a cluster of red hot pokers blooming wild that I knew from my mum's garden at home, and I remembered that a lot of flowers collected from South Africa way back in the day are now commonly found in gardens in the UK, and we don't ever think of them as being from elsewhere.

I was walking with scientists, and when I asked the name of a flower in one language they answered in another, and I had to ask them to repeat the names, and then for the spellings.

Disa graminifolia
Gladiolus monticola
Peucedaum

Hermas villosa
Disa uniflora

It's the translations from Latin that make more sense: the *Leucospermums* are the pincushions, masses of tiny pinhead flowers emanating from their inflorescence. A *Peucedanum galbanum* – that I was warned not to touch – is an innocuous-looking plant with leaves that look a bit like parsley, and is known as the blister bush because it irritates the skin. *Hermas villosa* is the tinderleaf, a plant with thick green leaves tinged with a velvety grey and almost furry on the underside – used, someone tells me, for lighting fires. I know that in this land of at least eleven languages[96] there will be other names that describe other attributes, applications and 'intrinsic values'.

We walked at a slow and steady pace, in silence, mostly, and in single file, and I couldn't imagine moving any faster in that heat. In the moment, and in a way, apart from the heat, it didn't feel all that different from walking in Scotland, except the swallows weren't quite the swallows I knew, nor the martins or swifts; and the scent, the quality of the air was just *different*. Eventually, after a couple of hours' trekking, we came to where the red disa were known to grow. They were tucked away, past their best, edging out from rocks and vegetation beside a small stream, behind and along from a waterfall at the aqueduct, where I replenished my water bottle with a tannin-stained trickle. These orchids, giant in relation to the other orchids of the fynbos, were just that little bit tired now, and there was not the display I'm told there sometimes is in other years. We walked along a stone wall, two feet wide, with a drop of two feet on one side and a drop of who knows what on the other, the fynbos rich and deep below us, and in amongst it a single, perfect specimen looked up towards us, impossible to get closer to. The lone call of a kind of shrike, a *bokmakierie,* cut the breeze – its name its sound.

Someone told me people make a pilgrimage to see these disas every year. They're special here, emblematic. Symbols on football and rugby team kits, on school and university badges. They flower at the end of the summer, and I wondered about what signals the change of season – swallows gathering on wires, thin strands of smoke on distant hills – and about the walks I take in Scotland during the solstices – the same hill, when I can. Something about marking a turn, the start of summer, the start of autumn, of a new phase of the year, of life. And, later, from the middle of the lockdown we found ourselves in, I'd think back and wonder if these walks to see orchids might have been the last walks out into the wild that some would have taken for quite some time.

Another day, three of us, with Naomi, one of SANBI's seed collectors, headed towards the coast, to False Bay, and parked behind a clutch of houses near a town called Glencairn, which I know of as a street in Pollokshields in Glasgow and a kind of whisky glass. I wonder how it came by its name. We started walking up a rocky, sandy track towards a hill called Elsie's Peak. Sugarbirds, the males' tails like streamers, called to each other from the tops of cone bushes, and swifts scoured the rocky promontory we'd walk around.

We were looking for *Polygala garcinii*, one of the plants on the target list Naomi carried, a low-growing plant with the common name of 'a dainty butterfly bush'. Somewhat tattered remnants of some flowers hinted at its prettiness, but by the time we were there, they sat unobtrusively, stems trailing and tangled, and we had to lift and shake them to see if any seeds fell into the hand we held below. Some of the plants had small, finely meshed bags over them, drawstrings tight around the stems, to gather the seeds as they fell – some seeds fall in the instant that they are ready and it's the only way to catch them. Gathering seeds can be an inexact science. You have to estimate the time from when the flowers bloom to when the seeds will be ready, and it's easy to be too early or too late, or to be busy doing something else and not get back to collect them in time, in which case it's another year's wait. For all the science, there's something intrinsically human about this process, something that is reassuringly slow and attentive and attuned to the seasons of the year. We found no more than ten or so seeds among the four of us, though more were gathered in the seed bags that had previously been placed over some of the flower heads.

We walked further up, curving over and round to a flatter area with a view to the north, and again wandered off the path. Next, we were looking for a rarer *Diastella*, and we spread out, combing the fynbos for these particular plants, low and sprawling, with occasional pink flowers. When we found them, we sat at different points across the hillside and searched individual plants. Naomi told us that the best chance of finding seeds would be from a flower that was in decline – at the stage just after the seeds have grown but before they have fallen. I'm sure I missed some with my unpractised hands, and they fell onto the ground to become the sandy, gritty soil beneath, until the next year at least, when, perhaps, they might just start to grow.

A rock kestrel flew over and alighted on a rock ledge, then sat quiet and still and watchful. Beyond False Bay the hills were shrouded in clouds brought by the southeasterly wind known as the Cape Doctor for its ability to blow away smog and cleanse the air. I was single-minded, focused on looking for one seed, then for another, then another; the sun was hot, but not too hot, and there was a light breeze. There I was, sitting in the middle of the fynbos in the far south of Africa, looking for things less than five millimetres in size, swallows flitting above.

That week, I also spent some time in the lab cleaning and processing the seeds. I spent hours with a set of tweezers, pulling the seeds from a dried-up flowerhead and separating them. When gathered, the sum of my labour was a cluster less than the size of a penny. I moved to sorting out the seeds of a species of *Helichrysum* that were around two millimetres in length, less than half a millimetre across, with longer, even thinner, stiff-looking white three-millimetre-long threads that emerged from the top, and which I imagined helicoptering in the lightest of breezes, attaching themselves to animals and people. When I looked through the microscope, their size and volume came into a three-dimensional hairiness that I could not quite see before. These tiny seeds looked like shuttlecocks, like spores, like the spokes of an umbrella blown out by the wind and with the canopy removed, so light they'd be borne by the wind and spread, relative to their size, over vast distances and land to start new life where they landed.

One afternoon, one of the Kirstenbosch horticulturalists, Mashudu, took me around an area known as the motherstock orchard (what a perfect name). He told me of seeds that were found in a leather wallet that had sat in the National Archives in London for over 200 years. Found by an archivist who was researching something entirely different, they had belonged to Jan Bekker Teerlink, a Dutch merchant whose boat, *The Henrietta*, had been captured by British privateers as it sailed from the Cape of Good Hope back to the Netherlands. Its cargo and documents were confiscated and passed to the British Admiralty where they remained before ending up in the UK National Archives. The seeds were passed on to botanists at Kew Gardens, who were able to germinate some of them using smoke, or rather, 'an aqueous smoke solution'.[97] One of the plants now grows in Kew Gardens. 'Imagine,' Mashudu said. 'These are seeds that haven't even been stored in the right conditions and look at what happened after all that time.' We just don't know what we will find with the seeds that we have and keep, and though we might assume seeds to have a longevity of ten to twenty years, clearly, there is hope on a much longer timescale. There are so many variables, so much that can change. Teerlink had carefully annotated the seeds he'd collected, using the Latin names and genuses as a possible start to identifying them when they were replanted, who knows where. In amongst the heaths and heathers that would remind me of my home and the sugarbushes that would not were others that he could only begin to describe:

Seeds from a tree with crooked thorns
Seeds from an unknown Mimosa

And:

Seeds of the wild water lemons whose fruits are eaten by the savages along the Orange river[98]

These little moments, fragments, words and opinions that reveal so much more and point to something else entirely.

It's hard to walk through the Kirstenbosch Garden, to be in Cape Town, in South Africa, and not acknowledge the racial-ised and politicised spaces we inhabit – even if there's nothing that sets where we are apart from the vaguest knowledge of history. It's the same in Glasgow, walking down Jamaica Street, Virginia Street and India Street. Glasgow's Gallery of Modern Art is on the site of what was the former mansion of a 'Tobacco Lord'. These are different geographies, held together by some of the same impetuses and predilections of colonialism, power and entitlement. Saidiya Hartman's notion of 'the afterlife of slavery' can take many forms and resonates in so many places across the globe. In Kirstenbosch, pre-dating the garden itself, are remnants of Jan van Riebeeck's hedge. Planted in the late seventeenth century, it acted as a boundary between a 'new' settlement forged by Dutch colonisers and the indigenous peoples who had lived and hunted in the area. 'For many,' the Kirstenbosch website tells us, 'this hedge marks the first step on the road to Apartheid and symbolises how white South Africa cut itself off from the rest of Africa, dispossessed the indigenous people and kept the best of the resources for itself.'

The District Six Museum in central Cape Town tells the history of how 60,000 people of colour were forcibly displaced during the Apartheid era. In the Slave Lodge, another of the museums of Cape Town dedicated to telling the histories of people and place in no uncertain terms, a map shows the forced migrations of those who were enslaved, those who contributed so much to the building of the city. Their stories, often just fragments, come together and reveal so much pain and loss and resilience. That map, with its swoops of arrows east to west, right to left, from India, Sri Lanka, the Indonesia archipelago, has that innocuous capacity that maps possess: to give so much information and yet so little. It doesn't look so different from those maps of bird migrations, sea currents and wind movements, or the maps that showed the initial spread of coronavirus.

It was strange to be 8,000 miles away from home and watch a virus spread across the world. How it moved east to west, but not quite south, not yet. The first cases in South Africa were identified a few days before I left. 'You're safe there,' people said, but I was more concerned about being so far away from home. It threw up all kinds of questions about safety, belonging and precarity that I was not expecting. In Cape Town, I was occasionally addressed in Afrikaans, and I have that same experience of an assumption that I am local, *from there*, when I visit the US, and it's not always clear that I am *not from there* until people hear my Scottish accent. There's always something nice about not feeling so different. You can forget, sometimes, that you can hold a tension without quite realising it, till something helps you let it go. Like how I used to feel when I went to London Pride or how I can feel walking through the forest or in the hills.

In the evenings back at the hotel, I'd keep an eye on the news and watch Covid-19's spread, the Johns Hopkins tracker showing the red dots expanding. I'd try to calibrate my life and plans when in Southern Africa with the quickening creep of Covid-19, concerned about the time I had left and whether I'd get to where I was supposed to be going. I watched, suddenly, Italy shutting down, airlines cancelling flights, a hotel quarantined in Tenerife, and the spread into Europe, and I fretted about returning home. The swallows were gathering themselves for their own journeys. Some would travel as far as Europe, perhaps Scotland, some to other parts of Africa. They'd travel their 200 miles, stopping at their resting points subject to the vagaries of wind and weather and changing agricultural practices, all of which year to year, might change the habitats so crucial for their sustenance, their survival.

A giant cycad grows in the Palm House at Kew Gardens and it's thought to be the world's oldest pot plant. It was collected from the Eastern Cape and brought back to the UK in 1775 by Francis Masson, a Scot originally from Aberdeen, who's described as being Kew's first plant collector. And I wonder at the term 'collector'. Sometimes they're described as explorers, or adventurers, plant gatherers, sometimes plant hunters, but never plant *takers* or thieves. 'Put on board a wooden sailing ship,' the Kew website tells me, 'the palm-like plant's long journey from South Africa to London would have taken several months. During the travels the cycad was strapped to the deck to give it access to rainwater and sunlight, before being transported by barge along the Thames to Kew.' A time-line sits alongside the cycad, detailing the world events that have occurred during this plant's lifetime:

1775   Cycad arrives at Kew
1804   Trevithick invents the first steam rail locomotive
1821   Constable paints *The Hay Wain*
1833   Abolition of slavery
1859   Darwin publishes *On the Origin of Species*

And I can't help but think that this plant was probably afforded more water and sunlight and respect than the human cargos transported at the same time and since. I think again about who can travel and how we do so, how we may move, how we might stay in place, and what might travel, what might move, what might take root, and what might prevent us from staying or going.

Table Mountain is the mountain that rises behind Cape Town. From some angles, it has a flat top. *Tafelberg* in Afrikaans, in Khoekhoe it's *Huriǂoaxa*, which means rising from the sea. It's all about perspective and where we stand; where we are placed or place ourselves affects what we see and how we see it.

In the end, I left Southern Africa earlier than I was meant to – only five days before South Africa placed travel restrictions on incomers from affected countries, before the world started to become even more worrisome, before lockdowns and social distancing and no one quite knowing where and how it would all end. I returned to a very different country from the one I'd left, with an awareness of my privilege as well as my vulnerability, aware of precarity in ways I've never thought about before. The country was in lockdown, and we were told to remain in our homes, and we waited and watched the world even as we waited and watched for the swallows to return.

oncoming

allerish	chilly; rather cold; *an allerish morning*
birssy	keen, sharp; *a birssy day*, a cold, bleak day
black-frost	frost without rime or snow lying on the ground, as opposed to white frost
blind, blin-drift	heavily driving snow, a blinding, drifting snow
caldrife, cauldrife	causing the sensation of cold; very susceptible of cold; indifferent, cool, not manifesting regard or interest; cold and rife; abounding in cold
cavaburd	a thick fall of snow
to chirl	to chirp; to emit a low, melancholy sound, as birds do in winter before a storm
cranrochie, craunrochie	rimy, abounding with hoar-frost
creep, cauld creep	that sensation of rigour which extends itself over the surface of the body in consequence of exposure to severe cold, or of some sudden alarm

crisp	a term used to denote the crackling sound made by the ground under one's feet, when there is a slight frost
to crump	to emit a crashing noise; to give such a sound as ice or frozen snow does, when it yields to the foot
dede-thraw	when the temperature of the atmosphere is in a dubious state between frost and thaw; the agonies of death
doon-fa'	a heavy fall of rain, snow
drift	flying snow, especially including the idea of its being forcibly driven by the wind; procrastination
eterie, etrie	keen, bitter, *an etrie sky*; ill-tempered; hot-headed; having an angry look
feeding storm	a fall of snow which is on the increase, and threatens to lie deep on the ground
feuchter	a slight fall of snow
flauchter, flauchlin, flaugh, flichen	a flake of snow
flist	a flying shower of snow; a fit of anger; a squall
floichen	an uncommonly large flake of snow or soot
frog	a flying shower of sleet or snow
girslin	a slight frost, a thin scuff of ice
glaisterie	*a glaisterie day,* one on which snow falls and melts

glottenin	a partial thaw, in consequence of which the water begins to appear on the ice
gull	chill, as in *a cauld gull nicht*, a chill evening; one marked by a cold wind
hair-frost	hoar frost
hullerie	raw, damp and cold
lamp	the ground is said to *lamp* when covered with the cobwebs which appear after dew or a slight frost
moorawav	a thick shower of snow
to nirl	to pinch with cold
pewil, pewl, peughle	used to denote the falling of snow in small particles, without continuation, during a severe frost
rhyne, rind, rynd	hoar frost
ringing black frost	a very severe frost, when the ground keeps black, and seems to ring when struck
skirl	wind accompanied by rain or snow, as in *a skirl o' snow*
skirvin	a thin coating of snow
to sloom	to become powerless; to become flaccid, applied to flowers and plants touched by frost
smore thow	a heavy snow, accompanied with a strong wind, which, as it were, threatens to *smore*, or smother one
snaw-brack	a thaw

snip, sneep, snippin	the dazzling of something white, as of snow
speen-drift	the snow when drifted from the ground by the wind
thirling	piercingly cold
unhearty	uncomfortable, as in *an unhearty day*; a day that is cold and damp; transferred to bodily feeling, when one ails a little, especially as regarding the sensation of cold
to waufle	to waver in the air, as snow, chaff or any light substance
yield	the influence of the sun on frost

kenspeckle   having so singular an appearance as to be recognised

THIS WINTER, THE SNOW FELL in bursts and lay for more than a couple of weeks, and there were days without more precipitation. Even though it felt so empty apart from occasional flurries of tits and finches, the snow betrayed the evidence of life and activity. Tiny vole or mouse tracks that barely indented the surface. Occasional holes where something had burrowed, or been hunting. One morning, there were tracks woven all around the house, close in, and into the porch, more scrabblings around the bird feeder and a spot where a little hole had been pawed out. We could see the track trace a line down from the hill and into the gap in the fence where the pine marten had come through. In the fields the distinctive tracks of brown hares, two feet together, one foot, then another, criss-crossed, and we could measure their activity in days, almost, the most recent indents bolder in relation to the fainter indents where their footprints had been snowed over. The hares seemed to vary their routes but nonetheless regularly came and went along and across the track to the field and the trees beyond. One night, the nature camera I'd set up pointing out to the field caught a hare crossing its field of view, then forty minutes later a fox passed in the same direction, and I wonder if it was tracking the former.

Once, we came across an unfamiliar set of prints up a forest track and, with nothing else to do, decided to follow them. They padded across a rickety, wee footbridge over the burn and on through the forest, past an enormous granny pine we hadn't encountered before, and then took us to a part of the forest we'd not been to. We scared up a bird from almost underfoot – maybe a woodcock, or perhaps (wishful thinking?) a capercaillie – that flew low and away so quickly that we could barely compute its presence. It sounded so loud because everything around us was so quiet. The snow was light and powdery, and as we looked in front of us we could see where the creature we were following had gone before we reached its tracks by seeing where it had brushed the snow from the heather. Eventually, and completely unexpectedly, about three-quarters of a mile on, we came across a badger sett where multiple sets of prints converged.

In the field behind the alder one morning, eight or nine patches of grass revealed where the snow had been melted or scraped away, hoof-prints visible to and from them. A herd of deer had eaten there, bedded down for a time, or both. A couple of nights after, there were more – this time six or seven patches of green marked the field to the south; these beasts had been close but completely unseen by us.

On one walk, we followed the path of a hare curving around the brow of a snow-bound field and saw when it had hopped, when it had bounded, and suddenly came across bird tracks that started suddenly and went in a line for three metres and stopped with a small loop that ended abruptly again. It was where one of the crows we'd seen at a distance had landed, walked a little, and taken off again. At the top of the field where it meets the forest, we have views back down and over the road to the woods closer to the house and up to a nearer ridge of hills. We're elevated just enough to see over to the northeastern Cairngorm mountains beyond. They're always snowier first, and the snow always stays there longer.

We can see over to Bynack More – a mountain of 1,090 metres that we've walked to, going along the track through the forest to its edges and beyond to the moorland now dotted with regeneration and slogging our way to the top. There's a point on the walk to the summit where the path forks off to the left (east), and if you were to take it, you'd go through the Lairig an Laoigh, an old drovers' road. Walking guides warn that the terrain is remote, bleak, and that a burn you have to cross to complete the route, if in spate, is impassable. There's a vulnerability I can feel in these places – a feeling of being just that little bit too far out and away, even though I know where I am. I get a fluttering in my chest that tells me in some existential way I'm outside my comfort zone and I feel slightly unnerved. The modern-day definition of uncanny can have associations with something that is unsettling and, perhaps, the supernatural. In old Scots it can also mean, variously: not safe, dangerous, awkward, inexpert, unlucky, unskilful, not deft, clumsy, careless. And I think somewhere in me there's a feeling of uncanniness that skips between each of these definitions – sometimes in the forest, definitely if I venture far up into the mountains. I default to a worry about getting lost (even if I'm sure where I am), falling, twisting my ankle or breaking my leg, so far away from help.

We try to get up onto the Cairngorm Plateau and to these bigger, more distant mountains a few times a year. The Cairngorm massif is the highest land area in the UK – the plateau is upwards of 1,000 metres, and the habitat has been described as having 'the most extensive range of arctic mountain landscape' in the UK. Winds whip up to over 150mph, windchill dips to minus twenty, and the snow can lie for months. There are plants up here that are found nowhere else in the UK, and birds you'd be hard pushed to see elsewhere: dotterel and snow buntings, unless they're on migration. These birds, with ptarmigan, the high-altitude cousins of the red grouse we see in the moorlands further down, all make their home here, and brown hares make way for the mountain hare. Both mountain hares and ptarmigan have adapted to these extreme environments for protection, in terms of their behaviour and how they look. The hare gains a thicker and denser winter undercoat, and the ptarmigan has thicker plumage and feathered feet. Without tree cover, or thick foliage for that matter, ptarmigan and hares have also resorted to other means of protection, using camouflage to protect themselves from those creatures who predate using sight. Nancy Jennings writes of the mountain hare: 'Its summer coat is brown with blue-grey underfur, but in winter it may remain brown, turn white or partly white, or turn blue-grey.'[99] How do these hares know when to change? Jackes and Watson observed that they turn back to brown more slowly in springs that are colder and have more snow than when it's milder, and other research has considered the seasonal shifts in a day's length/light as another variable.[100]

Ptarmigans also moult three times a year to better fit with the weather, and to be able to hide from visual predation their plumage turns white in winter. These birds, only found in the highest parts of Scotland, are thought to be amongst those species most vulnerable to climate change. Specialists of tundra and arctic-alpine vegetation and habitats, they have to survive in the most extreme conditions. The Scottish Ornithologists' Club says of the ptarmigan, 'It is isolated and sedentary, with no possibility of recruitment from abroad, so its conservation is a Scottish responsibility.'

The Scottish subspecies is recognised for adopting a more complete grey colour phase and keeping it longer, unlike most other subspecies that have more white flecks in their grey plumage and moult quickly into winter white. Some Scottish birds also retain more grey feathers throughout winter, from a few specks to heavily-freckled patterns, especially around the head in females. This plumage has probably evolved as a cryptic coloration adapted to the

Scottish mountains' sub-arctic/alpine and more oceanic climate with its more sporadic snow cover.[101]

How they blend with the grassy tussocks, the granite rock, the last patches of snow. There's a fear that as our climate changes and becomes potentially wetter and windier, mountain hares, ptarmigan and snow bunting will become more vulnerable, and we don't yet know how their camouflage strategies will cope and adapt, or how their food supply may alter. Recent research found that 'the camouflage mismatch of mountain hares is really surprising and worrying, and suggests that some wild animals can't adapt quickly enough to match the rate of climate change.'[102]

I wonder if hares and ptarmigan know the state they are in? How do they know where best to perch, where to land, to stand, and whether they're visible or hidden? I google 'bird camouflage' and come across an Audubon article, 'Are birds aware of their camouflage? A new study suggests so', which starts: 'Ground-nesting birds didn't just settle in spots that matched their species' markings – they hunkered down where their own patterns blended best.'[103]

When they are still, they are either so obviously out of kilter, or, if in synch, they are the granite, the snow-covered tussocks, the low-growing heath: impossible to see. We'll catch a movement out of the corner of our eye, or hear the ptarmigan startle and fly if flushed, then struggle to see it once it lands again.

These landscapes. You try not to think about the guddle and mess and tear of the ski slopes and the car park at the start of the walk, and walk away from it and up onto the plateau as quickly as you can. Once on the tops, even on the busiest of days, there's a vulnerability and overwhelmedness I feel that's completely in keeping with what these places are like and what they can demand. Looking south and over to the west, layers of mountains unfold and fade into sky. To the far north, if it's not too hazy, you can sometimes see as far as the Moray coast that Culbin curves along. Closer north and east, though, depending on where you are, you can see dots of pine green that thicken and conjoin to become a mass, and you look over and down and note how far the forest extends. Perhaps in twenty, forty, one hundred years, the mass will begin from higher up than it is now and extend further in all directions.

And, higher than you might think, you'll find the odd tree that has adapted to extremes, that seem very far out of its comfort zone. NatureScot describes these as krummholz-type Scots pine, and they're remnants of a habitat that's all but lost but attempts are being made to re-establish. The highest ones are stunted, crooked, low-growing – *Krummholz* is German for 'twisted wood'. Nan Shepherd of course describes this much more poetically, calling such trees 'out-liers' and writing: 'Gaunt remnants of pine trees high on the mountain sides show that the earlier forest went further up than the present forest does. Yet here and there a single seed, wind borne or dropped by a bird, has grown far above the main body of the trees.' Outliers.

THERE'S A HISTORY OF US dipping in and out of sight here in Scotland. Archaeologists from Historic Environment Scotland have found pottery that suggests some of the Roman soldiers stationed on the Antonine Wall may have been North African. The wall, the most northerly outpost of the Roman empire that cuts a line from east to west across Scotland's Central Belt, including just south of where the Forth and Clyde Canal would eventually wend, sits barely half a mile south of where my papa's father and grandfather were bridge-keeper and blacksmith.

There's the evidence of the 'moorish lasses' in the court of James IV (1473–1513) and in the eighteenth-century tapestry depicting the Battle of Culloden held by the National Trust for Scotland. The battle took place in 1746 and was the last stand of the Jacobites and Charles Edward Stuart. Tucked into the far right-hand side stands an unknown Black man, thought to be a servant of one of the officers (it would be a servant . . .). No one is quite sure who he is. I wonder how many people have looked at that tapestry without seeing him, how long he was there before he was noticed.

In 1756, and again in 1769, cases involving fugitives from slavery seeking freedom reached the Court of Session in Edinburgh – those of James Montgomery and David Spence – but both men died before a decision had been made. Joseph Knight was the third case to make it to Scotland's highest court. Born in West Africa, Knight had been enslaved in West Africa and taken to Jamaica, where he was sold to Sir John Wedderburn, a Scottish plantation owner, who eventually brought him to Scotland. Knight was in Wedderburn's household for years, then met and married a maid, Annie Thomson (Thomson!), who was dismissed from service when she became pregnant. When Wedderburn refused to let him live with his wife, Knight left Wedderburn's service, and Wedderburn had him found and arrested.

Knight sought to gain his freedom through the Scottish courts, arguing that as slavery was not recognised in Scotland, he essentially had been freed when he landed here. In 1778, after a series of cases and appeals, the Scottish Supreme Court ruled in favour of Joseph Knight and effectively ended legal slavery in Scotland.

James Robertson's historical novel *Joseph Knight* fictionalises Knight's life, and there's a part where, long after Knight has been a free man, Wedderburn tasks a man called Jamieson to find him. Jamieson returns with no news, saying, 'Were he yet in Dundee, I would hae discovered it. A black man in Dundee is a kenspeckle body. But as soon as ye reach Edinburgh, or the west, it's a different proposition . . .' Kenspeckle, *having so singular an appearance as to be recognised*. Where did Knight go? Where did he end up? What of his life after he won his case, and for others in the same position? Joseph, Annie and any children they had vanished from records after the court case was complete.

So much more is happening in Scotland now to take ownership of, and to admit culpability for, the country's involvement in Britain's colonial past. In the 'Runaway Slaves' project at the University of Glasgow, researchers found over seventy adverts from eighteenth-century Scottish newspapers.[104] Similar to adverts in the US, they offered rewards for the recapture of those who had fled their enslavement, seeking freedom, and not just in the cities, but in the Highlands and Islands as well. Often, Scots who had emigrated to work in sugar or tobacco, who'd 'made good' (for them) and built their fortunes on plantations, would bring back those they had enslaved as visual displays of wealth and status.

A MULATTO BOY, Yellowish colour, with only a short grey coat, vest and breeches of the same colour, without shoes or stockings. The name he went under was Sam, but some time names himself Donald; he has a squeaking voice; made his elopement from Balnaguard, in Athole, Wednesday the 11th September current, in the afternoon, and was seen on his way to Perth, above eight miles above that place. (*Edinburgh Evening Courant*, 1765)

So much of our history speaks to the presence of people of colour if we look long and hard enough, and a lot reveals the presence of racism, but it's without the experience, psychic or physical, of what it must have been like from the inside. We conjecture voices, but there are so very few real-life accounts.

I asked one of the historians involved in the 'Runaway Slaves' project whether they had further information about those named or described in these advertisements, those who fled enslavement, and was told that if they succeeded, they'd have disappeared from view, changed their names and appearance, travelling away from where they'd been held, having to actively avoid attention. And if any were recaptured or 'returned', we would not necessarily know – there'd be no adverts announcing this success (or failure, depending where you stand). We can conjecture, but not much more. I wonder how they managed to evade recapture, how easy it was for them to flee. Were they helped? What did those who they encountered think of these unco people? How were they able to get away, and where did they go? How was it to hide in plain sight, and how did they experience their freedom? And for those like me who were here, what was it like to be the Roman centurion, someone in the court of King James – to be someone who was able to flee or the child of someone who'd fled enslavement? Or someone of colour who just happens to have been, or be, here? Saidiya Hartman's 'afterlife of slavery' radiates back and forth and up and out, whether or not we ourselves feel part of the headline histories we're told.

We often think of the Highlands as the high lands – the

mountains, summits and plateaus that are so defining – but the ways through that were so vital for passage and transit are part of this place too. These passes, carved by glaciers and burns, cross boundaries and watersheds. Some form old drovers' roads with names like Calves' Pass, Thieves' Road, Smuggler's Path. Stories are told of cattle trysts being held in what for us today would be the most remote part of the glens, but back then these were the places where routes from east to west, north to south converged. Some paths took folk into the hills to their sheilings where their cattle and sheep were pastured in the summer. Others were longer, potentially more treacherous and, at points in the year, deadly. Until the 1870s the men of Rothiemurchus were tasked each spring with going through the Lairig Ghru, the most famous of the passes through the Cairngorms, clearing boulders that had been dislodged by winter's frost and snow.

For all that they are throughways, I like to think of them as escape routes too, for any who need them. I never would have thought, that day decades ago when I walked up Glen Tilt and saw the eagle and the peregrines, that if I'd kept going, I'd have reached the Lairig Ghru, and if I'd walked on, then on, I'd have reached where I am now.

In the decades since that day in Glen Tilt I've walked into a lot of those passes from different directions, sometimes crossing boulder fields, sometimes up through pinewoods and onto moorland, sometimes alongside rivers that will need forded some ways further up, but I've never walked from one end to the other – yet.

remaining state

ere-fernyear	the year before last
fairn-year	the past year
farn-year	the preceding year; last year
fern-year, -yer	the last or past year; a time that may never come
noo-a-days	now, in these days
lookin'-to	a prospect, future
onwaiter	a patient waiter for a future good
remaining state	a future state

O N SOME WINTER MORNINGS WHEN I was wee, we couldn't quite see outside because of the swirls of frost that patterned the insides of the bedroom window and the thicker ice in the corners that distorted the world. Every day, I'd walk to school and back – a good couple of miles each way – in snow or slush. I'd get home, hands and feet numb, cheeks burning from what Norman MacCaig calls 'winter's scalding sleet'. I'm sure I remember my gran putting out a basin of lukewarm water that felt like it was boiling, and I'd sit in the kitchen with my feet in it until they thawed out, and the pain would be even worse, for a time, than when they were frozen, and maybe then I'd have some of my gran's Scotch broth, a taste I can conjure to this day. I say that, though my mum doesn't remember any basins of water at all, which makes me wonder about my memory. But if it didn't happen, why would the idea even come into my head? Mum and I have more conversations now about how we don't remember and what we don't remember, and she puts it down to her age, but I think it's just who we are.

I have a recollection of photographs showing me thigh-deep in snow (aged three), knee-deep when older, wearing a duffel coat (was it, though?), mitts attached with wool through the coat sleeves so they wouldn't be lost (were they, though?).

When there was a white blanket of snow on the hills, I'd watch and wait and hope that the white would creep down and spread over the town, cancelling school. But really, how often did this happen? Once or twice a winter, or more often? How do we think back and where do we go with our thoughts? Is it just the headline days of school being off because of snow and going over the Couches sledging and falling into snowdrifts that sit brightly in amongst the more usual dreichness and wet and everyday greys? Maybe those photos were taken precisely because of something out of the ordinary, the usual weather and run-of-the-mill days interrupted by a moment of brilliant blue winter skies and a fall of snow so heavy that it dampened noise and stopped traffic and movement. Perhaps it's those images that amplify certain memories, in the same way as when stories that have been passed down orally are written or old folk songs sung through generations, once recorded, become reified and the version that is told.

In the way that summers seemed, in childhood, so consistently sunny and hot, and winters much more snowy, do we just remember more clearly the extraordinary? Do we just see and *mind* difference?

M<small>Y MUM ASKED HER OLDER</small> cousin – Aunt Liz's son – about his memories of the Haggs and what he remembers of his visits there. He doesn't remember much more than she does, though they can still reminisce. His wife dug out a picture of the auld hoose that they found when they cleared the house at Dennyloanhead when Aunt Liz died. They posted it to me, recorded delivery, and I scanned it and posted it back the same way, frightened it would get lost in the post. It feels somehow so precious to have, something more of a place that we thought was lost in time, and here we see, at the back, Lizzie (I recognise the eyes that looked out at me from an old auntie's face), Jean (with her determined mouth) and Wull (the ears), and in the front row, Bobby and Meg, my gran, though I can't see my gran in that wee lassie at all.

I RARELY GO DEEP INTO THE forest at night, though I sometimes stand on its edges and listen. I'll drive the ribbon of
road through the forest on my way home, always mesmerised
by the car headlights strobing the vertical lines of trees and
how what lies further away between and behind becomes a
void.

On the walk with my friend, counting regeneration, we
finished the last transect as dusk was falling. Suddenly, almost
imperceptibly, it became hard to see where I was walking or
even what was underfoot. A place that had been somewhat
familiar in daylight became uncanny. The contrasts and separ-
ations between sky and tree, air and solid, became indistinct as
night fell. As we walked back, eventually in near-darkness, to
where the car was parked, it was only in the last ten metres
that I realised where I was, and the quiet anxiety that had been
building within me in proportion to the fading light only
became apparent with the relief I felt when I knew where I
was again.

Once, at a symposium, I had a conversation with someone who mentioned a conference on Black women artists, and my first thought was that my work – about birds and forests and trees – wasn't about being a Black woman artist – though, as this is what I am, of course it is.

The time I watched the moth trap light up, I remember that the ferns around it seemed a brighter green than I had ever seen. I see then that I was interested in the space of light that came into the forest and what was drawn to that light. The night pushed in against my back with an almost physical presence, even as I faced towards the unnatural luminescence of the moth trap's lamp.

As I filmed the lamp coming on and gradually brightening, it was the first time I had stood in a forest at night and really thought about what it meant and how it felt. An anthropologist, Tim Ingold, writes about how we discover the world through movement,[105] but I know that's not always true. Instances of stillness and watching and waiting, moments consisting of pauses – and, to use David Bissell's term, 'rich durations'[106] – are intrinsic to how we act and how we come to learn about a place, and, I think, by extrapolation, how we come to know ourselves. It is often in stillness and quiet that a place, and who we are, can come to us most clearly.

After making the moth film, I went into the forest again at night, just to *see*. I set up a camera from a fixed point at the edge of the pinewood, pressed record, then wandered with a head torch, holding a smaller video camera to see how what was so familiar during the day might change. I saw – no, more *felt* – physically and psychically how alien, how othered it became for me. And how othered I myself became. I walked, then stood, with my back to a trunk of a Scots pine tree and waited to see if any moths would come (one or two smaller ones did, though I didn't linger long because midges began to flock, attracted by my breath). I walked around a birch tree, looking for moths and thinking that the moth known as the mottled beauty would blend effortlessly into the bark.

It was a moonless night with no landmarks or pointers except for the lights from the house, static and immovable, which rooted me and made me more comfortable in my wanderings, made me able to wander. The ground beneath me was full of presences – clumps of heather, entanglements of bracken that snared and snagged, moss-covered fallen trees. Absences too – the dips and pits and perforations of the understory that jarred and jolted like a last step down you didn't expect. My head torch formed a jerking pool of light that seemed to flit uncontrollably and made disproportionately large jumps compared to the shifts my head made in relation to where my feet met the ground. It was as if the torch mezzotinted the space, carving lightness from the dark, at least in brief.

That night, I felt a strange kind of disembodiment that came with an invisibility and a visceral separation of my head with my hands, my feet, and literally not quite knowing where to step. I think of the word proprioception:

Sometimes referred to as the 'sixth sense', proprioception includes the sense of position and movement of our limbs, the senses of muscle force and effort, and the sense of balance. These senses, triggered by our everyday activities, allow us to carry out our tasks successfully, without thinking . . . Our 'sixth sense' not only enables us to control the movements we make, but provides us with the ability to perceive ourselves moving in space and acting in relation to our surroundings.[107]

In the forest at night, these different parts of me became elements of self that I could now only see if I angled my head in a particular way, and if I looked to see where I was going, my body disappeared. I had to rely on the touch of footfall in a way I had to be more conscious of than if it was light and my eyes could do more of the work to mediate the ground and my tread with the rest of my body. Each step was tentatively negotiated through the heathery sponginess to what I hoped was solidity, and I had to guess how high I needed to raise my leg again after each step, stumbling forwards through space where I'd presumed heather would be growing.

As I looked at the raw footage of what I recorded, I had in my head the title of an exhibition by the artist Glenn Ligon, *We Had Everything Before Us – We Had Nothing Before Us*. I recalled seeing one of the coaldust text paintings in that exhibition, *Stranger in the Village #13*, at the Art Institute in Chicago, and it's a painting I've returned to look at more than once. In this work, Ligon responds to an essay where James Baldwin writes eloquently and powerfully on his experience of staying in a village in the Swiss Alps, where it became apparent to him that for many of the inhabitants it was the first time they had encountered a Black man. It's funny how thinking about the literal imposition of darkness, and blackness, made me more aware of myself than I'd been in a while, and I am still not sure where this quite takes me. I wonder if such a thing as psychic proprioception exists, or what that even might mean.

Ligon discusses Baldwin's essay with the writer Hilton Als, remarking that 'my sense is that he wouldn't have been able to stay there if psychically it was too much. If he hadn't been able to make sense of it in his writing.' And he talked about how and why Baldwin might 'choose to live there . . . choose to stay'.[108]

Odd memories leapfrog onto other, current, very different experiences, perhaps to haunt, perhaps just to remind, when they need to. Maybe it's because of the events in 2020 that brought to the fore the Black Lives Matter movement, or because I've recently re-read Claudia Rankine's book of essays *Citizen: An American Lyric*, in which she powerfully and poetically picks at the realities of race, visibility and invisibility, and the everyday disembodiment that occurs. Or it's just the way, and the reality, of things. Rankine writes:

> Even as your own weight insists
> you are here, fighting off
> the weight of nonexistence.[109]

From early on in my life, walking and birdwatching have provided me with a grounding and often, somehow, a solace, perhaps a place where I could be myself or I did not need to think about who I was, though I would not have been able to articulate that. But if I have a meditative practice, it's through walking, or standing looking for, or at, birds. I don't need to definitively know what I am looking at – sometimes the *perhaps* is enough, though the thrill of seeing another eagle, another diver, a ptarmigan, another crested tit, never goes away.

When I was a kid, growing up in my very own village in the unenlightened (and unendarkened) 1970s and 1980s, it always felt like I was the last person on the bus who someone would sit beside. When I was a kid, I would sometimes be taken aback when I caught my reflection in a window. Every summer, after folk had been to Spain for their holidays, some would come up and put their forearms next to mine, so they could compare, and say how much darker their skin had become next to mine. I still get taken aback when, even now, people feel they can come up to me and touch my hair; if they are polite, they'll ask first, and some will ask whether I wash it.

For many Black people growing up in the 1970s, *Roots* was their first reflection of self and history, but for me it was a surface rendition of difference that just gave people new words with which to articulate their ignorance. It broadened a language that they could use, and it became the source of *other* 'nicknames': Kunta Kinte one week, Kizzy the next.

Sometimes my white partner notices things that I have somehow become inured to. Did you see how that person stared? And we'll both notice when I ask someone a question and they respond to her.

I'm sure there was a point when I began to not notice things, or to only notice that which endangers me – physically or psychically. I think I choose to notice and ignore, without even realising I am noticing and ignoring. And I think of Claudia Rankine again. *Can we not just live our lives*. At least for some of the time. *Proprioception praejudicium*. What is the word for my brain and body's ability to sense where I am in the world: the ability that enables me to know where other people's perceptions of me are in space without having to look, and being able to deal with them accordingly, perhaps without realising that I am doing it? Do I do the same with sexism, homophobia? Claudia Rankine: 'That level of vigilance, I know from my own life, can drain you. It's easier to shut up and pretend it's not happening, as the bitterness and stress build up.' We all choose when and where we speak up, make a point, cast a look, and when we keep our own counsel. And when we do speak up, we'll think later about how we could have said what we said better, more trenchantly; or how, still, we're left flustered and feeling inarticulate, and wondering whether we over- or under-reacted. At the same time, I can snap, respond intuitively, viscerally. A casual racist comment as someone passes by will get a loud *fuck off* before I even think about whether I am endangering myself or not by reacting as I do.

In my late teens and early twenties I began to find and read the books and the grander narratives, mainly about the experiences of African Americans, that gave me insights not just about physical histories and outward discriminations but psychic perspectives too. If they did not exactly mirror my experience, then what resonated was often their anger, their explorations of difference, and sometimes the stories of hate, fear, ignorance, stupidity that can guide some people's lives and affect our own. Words took me beyond the well-meaning colour-blindness that had sometimes worked, sometimes hadn't. I found Alice Walker, Toni Morrison, read *The Color Purple*, *The Bluest Eye*, and colour itself became more vivid and more focused, and I read Audre Lorde and the anthology *This Bridge Called My Back*. I held the knowledge from these writers close and pocketed it away as part of me and my understanding of the world, instinctively, intuitively drawing on it, still, when occasions arise. Although I can't remember their specificities now, the nuances of these stories, these narratives gave me different worldviews that I could assimilate with my own experiences and helped me fathom them. I found bell hooks, who writes so powerfully on the margin as a site of creativity and power, and closer to home I found Maud Sulter and Sonia Boyce, and I heard Jackie Kay, who was the first voice who rooted me in *me*. Yet the first poet I ever heard read, Norman MacCaig, when I was a student at Edinburgh University, spoke as much to this other part of me, and I mind him still when I go walking and am awed, still, by these Highlands of Scotland. 'A swallow falls, and flickering through the barn, dives up again into the dizzy blue,' he writes in 'Summer Farm'. Later again, Nan Shepherd's *The Living Mountain* showed me the value of an intimate under-standing of place that went right into her bones and her being: 'Place and a mind may interpenetrate,' she writes, 'till the nature of both is altered.'

Walking in this forest during the day now, I am wholly myself: I am in my own body, my own skin. When I return after being away, I am often surprised – by how high the bracken grows, and so quickly; how you can hear a breeze coming before it arrives; by the seasonal shifting colours of larch and birch dotted between the constant, nuanced greens of the Scots pines. I'll hear the occasional call of crossbills and crested tits as they *flochter* from branch to branch. Sometimes, deer startle and run off, then they always seem to stop and look back at the source of their startlement, as if to check their reason for running, and I remember that a deer stalker once told me that it is in that moment that he can often take the shot. Blaeberry bushes are underfoot, and animal desire lines I can't help but follow, even if it is not quite the direction I intend to go. There's something timeless about being in these woods, right enough, and the constant process of growth, death, decay and regeneration are only vaguely palpable, but I see something different every time I'm there. Often, I feel like I am the only person there at all, and a noise, a whoosh, a bloodrush intermingles with the wind that shakes the branches and I begin to wonder anew if I know exactly where I begin, and where I am.

This never started out as a memoir, though perhaps it's become, in part, a memorial. Perhaps it is a re-rooting after moments of untethering, and a subtle re-gathering and re-placing. Even as I write and reread what I've written, I second-guess my memories, and stories can be reshaped to suit, and reshaped in every telling. Reading Claudia Rankine brings the subtleties of life and identity to the forefront of my mind in a way that I can often forget until I need to react, in the course of *just leading my life*.

In Kilsyth a lot of the countryside playgrounds of my youth have been paved and built upon. Old bluebell woods are no more. The Couches has a sprawl of new-builds that overlay the paths we used to walk over to the Stirling Road and the dam on our Sunday walks, where we used to sledge and roll Easter eggs, and where we'd go to pick blaeberries, so if we go for walks now, we have to take a different route. The Big Stane, the large boulder perhaps about six feet high with a side you could clamber up and a smooth side made shiny by the backsides of generations of Kilsyth children sliding down, is long gone. Papa's garden, the one next to the Castleview house that his sister sold to move to Stenhousemuir to find love, was sold when he got older and could no longer manage it. There's a house built on it now, though the old sandstone walls that surrounded the garden remain and mirror in kind the old house that still stands next door. I pass it on one of the routes into and out of the town, just before the canal, and it's funny, I feel more of a loss, or a welling, or some kind of nostalgia as I write about it here in a way I don't in the everydayness of passing it by. I wonder whether if I was to knock on the door of the new house and ask to walk around the garden with a metal detector, or if I was to dig a little ways down into the garden that remains, I'd come across something of my grandfather still; if any of the redcurrant bushes still climb up the inside walls, or whether any of his plant seeds even now lie dormant in the ground, waiting.

Still, now, when I go to that home, and go for walks out around the dam, or to the canal, sometimes it feels that not much is different, not that much has changed.

I finish writing this now in my house in the Highlands, in the middle of this forest that I walk in and talk to and which speaks back to me, but on its own terms, without judgement or bias. I have spent the last few days here by myself, and on Tuesday night there was a thunderstorm so present and insistent that I got up from the bedroom and went downstairs. A sudden, fierce wind brought a deluge, and lightning lit the forest as if it were day: but in the morning, I could see no damage.

This is where I choose to live, choose to stay.

ACKNOWLEDGEMENTS

A number of people have helped the writing of this book, and heartfelt thanks must go . . .

To my wonderful agent, Laura Macdougall, her assistant Olivia Davies, and Jim Gill at United Agents, for all the work they do for us all.

To my original editor at Canongate, Megan Reid, for her thoughtful edits and comments, and to Simon Thorogood who picked up where she left off, and to Vicki, Melissa, Caitriona, Aisling, Jenny and all the team at Canongate.

The original genesis for some of this writing came from my PhD, and thanks must go to the University of the Highlands and Islands, Forestry and Land Scotland and Highlands and Islands Enterprise who supported my studies. Thanks also to staff and volunteers past and present at RSPB Abernethy reserve and the Forestry Commission, including Desmond Dugan, now a friend and neighbour as well as someone who knows his fishing flies.

Thank you also . . .

Becks Denny, who let me walk with her, looking for cross-bills and counting regeneration, and to her and her family for their friendship and letting us house-sit and stay for all these years before we became neighbours.

Jessica J. Lee for her support, the stellar work she does with *The Willowherb Review*, and for her careful reading of the manuscript.

Kathleen Jamie for her gentle support, encouragement, and for showing me the possibilities for my own writing through her own work.

Edinburgh International Book Festival for inviting me to be part of their Outriders Africa project, and Victoria and her team at the South African National Biodiversity Institute, who so generously hosted me when I was in Cape Town.

Ruth Little, for her invitation to be part of the Cape Farewell project, which resulted in the trip to Mingulay, and for her abiding friendship afterwards.

Simon Newman and Karly Kehoe, so instructive for the conversations we had around the University of Glasgow's Runaway Slaves project, and about people of colour in the Scottish Highlands.

Paul at the Forth and Clyde Canal Society was incredibly generous for sending me old photographs of Auchinstarry, and finding the transcript of the interview with my papa, which must be over 40 years old.

Gavin from the Royal Scottish Forestry Society, for finding me the Dixon article when I had long lost my original copy.

Miss Jack and Duggie MacInnes, the teachers that got me through, and my pals from sunny Kilsyth.

And, of course, EKR, for her unwavering encouragement, belief and support, for always being there as the first pair of editorial eyes, and to my family, and the stories gathered and the stories told.

Some versions of some of the pieces in this book have appeared in other publications in various shapes and sizes, including the journals *The Willowherb Review*; *Gutter*; *The Irish Pages*; and the anthologies *Shared Stories: A Year in the Cairngorms* (Cairngorm National Park Authority); *Antlers of Water: Writing on Nature and the Environment of Scotland* (Canongate); *The Wild Isles: An Anthology of the Best of British and Irish Nature Writing* (Head of Zeus)

This book is about Scotland and the landscapes of Scotland. I'd like to thank some of the musicians whose music so often accompanies me when I'm working and going up and down and up and down the A9 and beyond, and so speaks to the places that I love: Lauren MacColl, Rachel Newton, Salt House, Duncan Chisholm, Breabach, Diamh, Kinnaris Quintet, Ross & Ali, Maireared Green and so many more trad musicians and bands too numerous to mention.

SOURCES

Throughout . . .

Jamieson, J.J. *A Dictionary of the Scottish Language*, abridged from the Dictionary and Supplement, in four volumes quarto, by John Johnstone. Edinburgh: William Tait, 1846.

Warrack, Alexander. *A Scots Dialect Dictionary, Comprising the Words in Use from the Latter Part of the Seventeenth Century to the Present Day.* Edinburgh: W. & R. Chambers, 1911.

PROLOGUE

1 Steven, H.M. and Carlisle, A. *The Native Pinewoods of Scotland.* Edinburgh: Oliver & Boyd, 1959.

PART I

2 Warrack, *A Scots Dialect Dictionary.*

3 hooks, bell. 'Choosing the Margin as a Space of Radical Openness'. *Framework: The Journal of Cinema and Media*, 36 (1989).

4 Crenshaw, Kimberlé. 'Demarginalizing the Intersection of Race and Sex: A Black Feminist Critique of Antidiscrimination Doctrine, Feminist Theory and Antiracist Politics'. *University of Chicago Legal Forum*, Vol. 1989 Issue 1. And see article on

Crenshaw: 'The woman who revolutionised feminism and landed at the heart of the culture wars', *The Guardian*, 12 November 2020.

5 Morrison, Toni. *Beloved*. London: Picador, 1988.

6 Evaristo, Bernardine. *Girl, Woman, Other*. London: Hamish Hamilton, 2019.

7 Anaxagorou, Anthony. *After the Formalities*. London: Penned in the Margins, 2019.

8 Morrison, Toni. 'Peril', *Mouth Full of Blood: Essays, Speeches, Meditations*. London: Chatto & Windus, 2019.

9 Shepherd, Nan. *The Living Mountain*. Edinburgh: Canongate, 2008.

10 Rankine, Claudia and Loffreda, Beth. *The Racial Imaginary: Writers on Race in the Life of the Mind*. Hudson, NY: Fence Books, 2015.

11 Weidensaul, Scott. *Living on the Wind*. New York: Farrar, Straus & Giroux, 1999, p. 47.

12 Groome, Francis H. *Ordnance Gazetteer of Scotland: A Survey of Scottish Topography, Statistical, Biographical and Historical, Volume IV*. Edinburgh: Thomas C. Jack, 1885.

13 Dennison, E. Patricia, Ewart, Gordon, Gallagher, Dennis and Stewart, Laura. *Historic Kilsyth: Archaeology and Development*. York: Council for British Archaeology, 2006.

14 Scottish Rights of Way and Access Society, Heritage Paths project. See Old Coach Road, Kilsyth, to Auchinstarry: http://www.heritagepaths.co.uk/pathdetails.php?path=399.

15 Groome, *Ordnance Gazetteer of Scotland*.

16 *Abernethy National Nature Reserve – Management Plan, Vision (2010–15)*. RSPB, 2010.

17 Wilkinson, Nick. RSPB National Capercaillie Survey 2015–2016. See https://community.rspb.org.uk/ourwork/b/biodiversity/posts/national-capercaillie-survey-2015-16.

18 Summers, Ron W. *Abernethy Forest: The History and Ecology of an Old Scottish Pinewood*. The RSPB Centre for Conservation Science, 2018.

19 Summers, *Abernethy Forest*.

20 Dixon, G.A. 'Forestry in Strathspey in the 1760s', *Scottish Forestry*, 30, 1976.

21 Smout, T.C. *Exploring Environmental History: Selected Essays*. Edinburgh: Edinburgh University Press, 2009.

22 Steven and Carlisle. *The Native Pinewoods of Scotland*.

23 Dixon, 'Forestry in Strathspey in the 1760s'.

24 Smout, T.C. 'The Pinewoods and Human Use, 1600–1900', *Exploring Environmental History*.

25 Steven and Carlisle. *The Native Pinewoods of Scotland*.

26 Forsyth, The Reverend W. *In the Shadow of Cairngorm: Chronicles of the United Parishes of Abernethy and Kincardine*. Inverness: The Northern Counties Publishing Company, 1900.

27 Cairngorms Connect, http://cairngormsconnect.org.uk

28 *Culbin: Britain's Forests*, Forestry Commission pamphlet, 1949.

29 Steers, J.A. 'The Culbin Sands and Burghead Bay'. *The Geographical Journal*, Vol. 90 No. 6, 1937.

30 Forestry Commission Scotland, Culbin Design Plan, 2011.

31 British Geological Survey Aviemore Scotland Sheet 74E. Solid Geology. 1:50000. Keyworth, Nottingham: British Geological Survey, 1993.

32 Steers, J.A. 'The Culbin Sands and Burghead Bay'.

33 McCallum-Webster, Mary, 'Plant Life', *The Moray Book*, Donald Omand (ed.), Edinburgh: Paul Harris Publishing, 1976.

34 Bachelard, Gaston. *The Poetics of Space*. New York: Orion Press, 1964.

35 Solnit, Rebecca. *A Field Guide to Getting Lost*. Edinburgh: Canongate, 2006.

36 Forrester, Ron and Andrews, Ian (eds). *The Birds of Scotland*. Edinburgh: Scottish Ornithologists' Club, 2007.

37 Holmes, Bob. 'If you think a crow is giving you the evil eye . . .'. *New Scientist*, 2745, 26 January 2010.

38 Swift, Kaeli N. and Marzluff, John M. 'Wild American crows gather around their dead to learn about danger'. *Animal Behaviour*, Vol. 109, November 2015.

39 Gilmour, David. *Reminiscences of the 'Pen' Folk. By One Who Knew Them*. Edinburgh: Edmonston & Douglas, 1873.

40 Hume Brown, P. *A Short History of Scotland*. Edinburgh: Oliver & Boyd, 1908.

41 Hear the tunes on Malinky's *3 Ravens* (2002) or Tannara's *Trig* (2016).

42 Gordon, Seton. *Hill Birds of Scotland*. London: Edward Arnold & Co., 1915.

43 Forrester, Ron and Andrews, Ian (eds). *The Birds of Scotland*.

PART II

44 Weidensaul, *Living on the Wind*.

45 Gange, David. *The Frayed Atlantic Edge: A Historian's Journey from Shetland to the Channel*. London: William Collins, 2019.

46 hooks, bell. *Feminist Theory: From Margin to Center*. London: Pluto Press, 2000.

47 Gordon, Seton. *Hebridean Memories*. Dumfries: Neil Wilson Publishing, 1995.

48 Stewart, Angus and Hansom, James D. 'Tir a'mhachair, tirnan

loch? Climate change scenarios for Scottish Machair Systems: A wetter future?', Scottish Natural Heritage, 2009.

49 Buxton, Ben. *Mingulay: An Island and Its People*. Edinburgh: Birlinn, 1995.

50 Stewart, Susan. *The Poet's Freedom: A Notebook on Making*. Chicago: University of Chicago Press, 2011.

51 See British Trust for Ornithology: https://www.bto.org/our-science/projects/ringing/surveys/ces.

52 Solnit, *A Field Guide to Getting Lost*.

53 Hartman, Saidiya. *Lose Your Mother: A Journey Along the Atlantic Slave Route*. New York: Farrar, Straus & Giroux, 2007.

54 Kay, Jackie. *Red Dust Road*. London: Picador, 2010.

55 Hartman, *Lose Your Mother*.

56 Eddo-Lodge, Reni. *Why I'm No Longer Talking to White People About Race*. London: Bloomsbury Circus, 2017.

57 Interview with Claudia Rankine, 'Blackness in the white imagination has nothing to do with black people', *The Guardian*, 27 December 2015.

58 Morrison, 'Peril', *Mouth Full of Blood*.

59 Rankine and Loffreda, *The Racial Imaginary*.

60 Kay, *Red Dust Road*.

61 Fusco, Coco. *The Bodies That Were Not Ours And Other Writings*. London/New York: Routledge, 2001.

62 RSPB press release on the capercaillie being under serious threat, 20 April 2011: http://ww2.rspb.org.uk/about-the-rspb/about-us/media-centre/releases/278165-capercaillie-continue-to-struggle.

63 Cairngorms National Park article on the decline of the capercaillie population, 4 June 2021: https://cairngorms.co.uk/new-lek-data-reveals-challenges-for-capercaillie/.

64 Gordon, *Hill Birds of Scotland*.

65 Nethersole-Thompson, Desmond and Watson, Adam. *The Cairngorms: Their Natural History and Scenery*. London: Collins, 1974.

66 Thomson, Amanda. *A Scots Dictionary of Nature*. Glasgow: Saraband Books, 2018. Oxford English Dictionary: www.oed.com. Tate online glossary of art terms: https://www.tate.org.uk/art/art-terms. Wikipedia.

67 Nethersole-Thompson and Watson, *The Cairngorms*.

68 See http://pza.sanbi.org/vegetation/fynbos-biome.

69 Forsyth, *In the Shadow of Cairngorm*, p. 297.

70 Dixon, 'Forestry in Strathspey in the 1760s'.

71 Shepherd, *The Living Mountain*.

72 Summers, *Abernethy Forest*.

73 NatureScot Trend Note, 18 April 2019, 'Trends of Moths in Scotland': https://www.nature.scot/trend-notes-scottish-moths. The authors note: 'Moths make up an important part of Scotland's biodiversity with about 1,300 species known and have high potential to be used as an indicator to measure progress in conserving Scotland's biodiversity.'

74 See 'Why moths matter', Butterfly Conservation: https://butterfly-conservation.org/moths/why-moths-matter.

75 See 'The state of Britain's butterflies', Butterfly Conservation: https://butterfly-conservation.org/butterflies/the-state-of-britains-butterflies.

76 See 'Moth conservation', Butterfly Conservation: https://butterfly-conservation.org/moths/moth-conservation.

77 Lammas is 1 August.

78 In episode 392 of the podcast, *99% Invisible*, Andrew Blum talks

about his book *The Weather Machine* (New York: Ecco Press, 2019) https://99percentinvisible.org/episode/the-weather-machine/.

79 The Long Now Foundation was established in 01996 to foster long-term thinking and responsibility in the framework of the next 10,000 years. See https://longnow.org/.

80 See Bulletin of the Atomic Scientists: https://thebulletin.org/doomsday-clock/.

81 See 'Doomsday clock lurches to 100 seconds to midnight – closest to catastrophe yet', *The Guardian*, 23 January 2020. It remained at 100 seconds to midnight in 2021.

82 *Lewis, Simon L. and Maslin, Mark A., 'Defining the Anthropocene'*, *Nature*, 11 March 2015: https://www.nature.com/articles/nature14258.

83 See 'The Anthropocene epoch: scientists declare dawn of human-influenced age, *The Guardian*, 29 August 2016.

84 Smout, T.C. *A Century of the Scottish People: 1830–1950.* London: Fontana Press, 1997.

85 Yusoff, Kathryn. *A Billion Black Anthropocenes or None.* Minneapolis: University of Minnesota Press, 2018.

86 Yusoff, *A Billion Black Anthropocenes or None.*

87 Yusoff, *A Billion Black Anthropocenes or None.*

88 Yusoff, *A Billion Black Anthropocenes or None.*

89 Yusoff, *A Billion Black Anthropocenes or None.*

PART III

90 Grahame, James. *The Birds of Scotland, With Other Poems.* Boston: S.F. Bradford, 1807.

91 Wernham, Chris et al (eds). British Trust for Ornithology. *The Migration Atlas: Movements of the Birds of Britain and Ireland.*,

London: T. & A.D. Poyser, 2002.

92 See 'Hirundinidae – Swallows and Martins', British Trust for Ornithology: https://www.bto.org/understanding-birds/birdfacts/bird-families/swallows.

93 See UNESCO Cape Floral Region Protected Areas: https://whc.unesco.org/en/list/1007/.

94 Victoria Wilman gave me a PDF of her talk, 'Ex-situ conservation in South Africa', presented at the International Symposium of Korea National Arboretum, 2019. See also https://www.kew.org/science/our-science/projects/national-seed-collection-south-africa.

95 From an information sheet that Victoria Wilman sent me: SANBI Biodiversity Fact Sheet 8, *Threatened Species*.

96 South Africa's Constitution recognises eleven languages, though there are many more.

97 Daws, Matthew I. et al. 'Two-hundred-year seed survival of *Leucospermum* and two other woody species from the Cape Floristic region, South Africa'. *Seed Science Research*, Vol. 17 Issue 2, June 2007.

98 Daws, Matthew I. et al, 'Two-hundred-year seed survival'.

99 Jennings, Nancy. *RSPB Spotlight: Hares*. Sandy: RSPB, 2017.

100 Jackes, Anne D. and Watson, Adam. 'Winter whitening of Scottish Mountain hares (*Lepus timidus scoticus*) in relation to daylength, temperature and snow-lie', *Journal of Zoology*, 2009.

101 Forrester and Andrews, *The Birds of Scotland*.

102 'New research shows increased camouflage mismatch in mountain hares due to climate change', The James Hutton Institute: https://www.hutton.ac.uk/news/new-research-shows-increased-camouflage-mismatch-mountain-hares-due-climate-change.

103 'Are birds aware of their camouflage? A new study suggests so', Audubon: https://www.audubon.org/news/are-birds-aware-

their-camouflage-new-study-suggests-so

104 https://www.runaways.gla.ac.uk

105 Ingold, Tim. *Being Alive: Essays on Movement, Knowledge and Description*. London: Routledge, 2011.

106 Bissell, David. 'Animating suspension: waiting for mobilities'. *Mobilities* Vol. 2 Issue 2, 2007.

107 Gandevia, Simon and Proske, Uwe. 'Proprioception: the sense within', *The Scientist*, 2016: https://www.the-scientist.com/features/proprioception-the-sense-within-32940

108 Glenn Ligon. *Yourself in the World: Selected Writings and Interviews*. New Haven: Yale University Press, 2011.

109 Rankine, Claudia. *Citizen: An American Lyric*. Minneapolis: Graywolf Press, 2014.

IMAGE CREDITS